D0989413

I

Stories That Make the World

The
Civilization
of the
American Indian
Series

Okanagan Lake, British Columbia.

I

Stories
That Make
the World

Oral Literature
of the Indian Peoples
of the Inland Northwest

As Told by
Lawrence Aripa,
Tom Yellowtail,
and Other Elders

Edited by
Rodney Frey

WITHDRAWN
Rock Valley College
Educational Resources
Center

University of
Oklahoma Press
Norman and London

Also by Rodney Frey

The World of the Crow Indians: As Driftwood Lodges (Norman, 1987)
Eye Juggling: Seeing the World Through a Looking Glass and a Glass Pane (Lanham, Maryland, 1994)

All royalties from the sale of this book go to the storytellers.

Library of Congress Cataloging-in-Publication Data

Stories that make the world : oral literature of the Indian
  peoples of the Inland Northwest as told by Lawrence
  Aripa, Tom Yellowtail, and other elders / edited by Rodney
  Frey.
      p. cm.—(The civilization of the American Indian
  series : v. 218)
    Includes bibliographical references and index.
    ISBN 0-8061-2710-4 (alk. paper)
    1. Indians of North America—Northwest Coast of
  North America—Folklore. 2. Oral tradition—Northwest
  Coast of North America. I. Frey, Rodney, 1950– .
  II. Series.
  E78.N78S766 1995
  398.2'089'970795—dc20   94-39935
                                        CIP

Text design by Cathy Carney Imboden.

Stories That Make the World: Oral Literature of the Indian Peoples of the Inland Northwest. As Told By Lawrence Aripa, Tom Yellowtail, and Other Elders is Volume 218 in The Civilization of the American Indian Series.

The paper in this book meets the guidelines for permanence and durability of the Committee on Production Guidelines for Book Longevity of the Council on Library Resources, Inc. ♾

Copyright © 1995 by the University of Oklahoma Press, Norman, Publishing Division of the University. All rights reserved. Manufactured in the U.S.A.

1 2 3 4 5 6 7 8 9 10

E
78
N78
S766
1995

To the storytellers

May that which is
most cherished and sacred
continue to be heard and lived
—the stories.

Contents

I

Illustrations

Map

Preface

As a member of my school district's Language Arts Curriculum Committee in Coeur d'Alene, Idaho, I was helping review various anthologies and trade books for districtwide adoption. It was at an early stage in the process that an intriguing and, what has turned out to be, critical set of questions arose. The textbook representatives who came before our committee each assured us that, among other things, their books contained "authentic" literature reflecting the primary and unaltered works of the selected authors. Of the reviewed texts, most were written with imagination and were wonderfully illustrated. Above all, the texts seemed "inviting," framed in the literary and thematic sensibilities and in modes of expression with which our students could readily identify.

My own contribution to the review process focused on multicultural literature—especially the myths, legends, and tales emanating out of the oral traditions of the American Indian. With reference to these materials, several questions arose:

> Were the myths and legends indeed "authentic"? Who were their "authors"? Did they reflect the particular cultural orientations and express the specific literary themes unique to that literature? Did the written account of a legend, revisited in solitude as an object on the pages of a book, convey the same meanings and spirit that it had when shared in conversation with others as an event within the oral tradition from which it emanates? In other words,

just whose sensibilities and modes of expression were conveyed in the stories under review?

The significance of the distinction between the oral stories as told in their indigenous settings and as published in written accounts first became apparent to me after hearing various Crow Indian storytellers. Experienced in their traditions and in the techniques of telling, the storytellers shared their stories with much animation, with "life." I once had the privilege of hearing several episodes from the story of Curtain Boy and Spring Boy. We were so engaged in the story that we all lost track of time. It was only when the storyteller's son came to "fetch" him for a feast that the spell was broken. After the telling, we consulted the written account of the same story, originally published some seventy years prior.[1] Common literary motifs and cultural themes were readily apparent in both the oral telling and the written account. But significantly, what differed were their contrasting formats and my involvement in the stories. In the oral presentation, in a fashion I am only now beginning to comprehend, I *participated* in the story. The characters were alive. They danced before me, and I before them. I became part of the story. The literary themes and the text formats represented in the written account versus the oral presentation of the stories suggested two differing literatures.

The Language Arts Curriculum Committee decided to seek the assistance of our neighbors, the Coeur d'Alene Indian people, where an oral literature continues to be told and is at the "heart" of the people. After consulting with their Culture Committee and gaining endorsement for the preparation of a Coeur d'Alene literature curriculum component, I was led into the living culture of the Coeur d'Alenes. To appreciate the significance of their stories, they told me, "You first have to get to know us as a people." I had afternoon conversations with elders, participated in powwow celebrations, and shared in Sweat Lodge rituals. With the generous assistance of the Coeur d'Alene elders and with funding from the Idaho Humanities Council, a Coeur d'Alene Indian oral literature component was adopted by the school board and incorporated into the school district's language arts curriculum. Elders came to the city's schools and brought their stories to life. Written transcriptions, reflecting the oral nuances of the telling, were made and disseminated. These stories appear in the fourth grade text and on a videotape, both entitled, *Me-y-mi-ym: Oral Literature of the Coeur d'Alene Indian People.* An introduction to the oral literature of Indian peoples, *Stories That Make the World,* was also written and made available as a general background guide for the teachers of the school district. The guide was intended to provide classroom teachers with a context for better understanding the particular Coeur d'Alene narratives incorporated into the school district's curriculum. In addition to the background materials provided by the Coeur d'Alenes, *Stories That Make the World* also relies on the oral literature of the Crow of Montana and other peoples of the region. As a result of this project, an Indian oral literature, sophisticated and rich in expressiveness and creativity, is now heard and read along with other works of literature in the Coeur d'Alene School District, a district of non-Indian students, and in the schools on the Coeur d'Alene Indian Reservation.

This published edition of *Stories That Make the World* incorporates the materials originally appearing in the teacher's guide, along with a series of photographs and additional stories. The photographs offer visual imagery for many of the natural and geographic features referred to in the stories, especially the rivers and the lakes. It is truly a mythic landscape within which the stories are embedded. I have also added two Coeur d'Alene stories to the four Lawrence Aripa had previously shared, a Kootenai story as told by Basil White, and four additional Crow stories as told by Tom Yellowtail.

Stories That Make the World is thus an attempt at addressing the question of authenticity and fostering

The Columbia River Gorge near Biggs, Oregon, 1955. (Photo by Edwin Roby)

an appreciation of the stories of Indian peoples in a manner the original storytellers intended. It seeks to place an oral literature in its cultural, literary, and expressive context. I hope I have accomplished this in a manner that renders the literature accessible to a wide audience, literature free from "overtranslation" and technical jargon, literature alive with the "heart" of a people.

Acknowledgments

*A*mong *those who* have told their stories with beauty and vigor, and to whom I owe sincere gratitude, are Tom and Susie Yellowtail and Alan Old Horn of the Crow; Lawrence Aripa, Cliff SiJohn, and Bingo SiJohn of the Coeur d'Alene; Vic Charlo of the Bitterroot Salish; Basil White of the Kootenai; Mari Watters of the Nez Perce; and Clarence Woodcock of the Pend d'Oreille. I hope that in this endeavor I have rewarded their trust..

A special thanks goes to Francis SiJohn for providing the Coeur d'Alene terms that appear in this work. They reflect the Coeur d'Alene language as it is spoken in the "mountain country," the northern region around the Cataldo Mission and Lake Pend Oreille, not in the southern area around the St. Joe River. The particular spelling of the Coeur d'Alene as well as the Crow terms that appear in this work are indicative of language texts developed for and used in the schools on each of the two reservations.

In helping to convey the life of these stories to those of us grounded in a literate society, I am indebted to the pioneering works of Dell Hymes and Dennis Tedlock, both linguistic anthropologists. They, more than any others, have provided the invaluable theoretical foundation and technical methodology for the interpretation and presentation of American Indian oral literature. Dell's specific comments on "The Couple Befriended by the Moon" narrative and on the Orality and Literacy section in the third chapter were greatly appreciated. I also wish to thank Karl Kroeber for his helpful suggestions on the entire manuscript and for his particular comments on the "Coyote and the Swallows" story.

The title for this work was originally suggested by Bruce Wallenberg, director of the Idaho Institute of Christian Education. When he asked me to give a presentation on American Indian oral literature at the University of Idaho's Campus Christian Center, Bruce entitled the talk, "Stories That Make the World." What more appropriate title for a work that introduces many of the creation stories of the American Indian and the notion that, in the act of storytelling, the stories indeed "make the world"? Thank you, Bruce.

The teacher's guide for this book could not have been written without the generous support of the Idaho Humanities Council and the Coeur d'Alene School District. I owe special appreciation to Chris Bain and Ron Fisher, both teachers within the district. For their editing comments, thanks go to Linda Erickson and Ursula Smith. I am particularly indebted to the Coeur d'Alene Tribe Culture Committee, to Cliff Si-John, Alfred Nomee, Dixie Saxon, Mariane Hurley, and Ernie Stensgar, the tribal chairman. They brought me into their Family, their Powwow, and their Sweat Lodge, and shared their "hearts" with me.

For permission to reprint copyrighted materials in a reformatted, "poetic" style, I am grateful to the American Folklore Society ("Sweat Lodge" from Verne Ray's "Sanpoil Folk Tales," *Journal of American Folklore Society* 46, 1933; and the "Coyote and the Swallows," "Elk and the Young Man," and "Seal Boy" from Edward Sapir's "Wishram Texts," *Journal of American Folklore Society* 41, 1909); to the Regents of the University of California and the University of California Press ("Two Coyotes" from Haruo Aoki's *Nez Perce Texts* 1979 and "The Couple Befriended by the Moon" from Robert Lowie's *Crow Texts* 1960); to Holt, Rinehart, and Winston (Robert Lowie's "The Old Man Coyote and his Dart" [retitled "Coyote and the Dart" in this volume] from *The Crow Indians*, 1935, [renewed by Lovella Cole Lowie in 1963]); and to the University of Washington ("Coyote and the Sweat Lodge" from Melville Jacobs' *Northwest Sahaptin Texts* 1929). No further reproduction of these materials is allowed.

For permission to use the following photographs, I am grateful to the Idaho State Historical Society: "Post Falls" (acc. no. 78-37.59) and from the Jane Gay photo collection, "Salmon Feast" (acc. no. 63-221.221), "Heart of the Monster" (acc. no. 63-221.60), and "Pipe and Tobacco Bag" (acc. no. 63–221.183). I also thank Jane Fritz and Edwin Roby for use of their photographs.

RODNEY FREY

I

Stories
That Make
the World

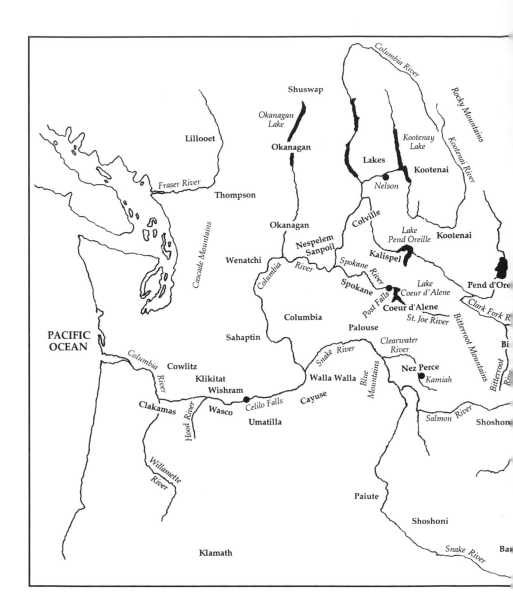

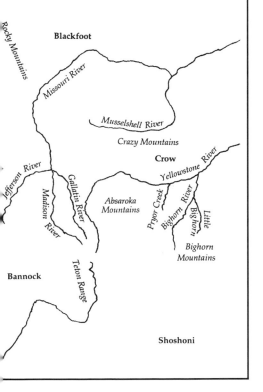

Indian Peoples
of the Inland Northwest

Rocky Mountains

Blackfoot

Missouri River

Musselshell River

Crazy Mountains

Crow

Yellowstone River

Jefferson River

Gallatin River

Madison River

Absaroka Mountains

Pryor Creek

Bighorn River

Little Bighorn

Bighorn Mountains

Bannock

Teton Range

Shoshoni

Indian peoples of the
Inland Northwest.

I

Introduction

"The Tin Shed"

It was a warm and pleasant June afternoon. We sat on a wooden bench, worn with use, under the shade of a huge cottonwood. I was interviewing an elder, Alan Old Horn, as part of an ethnographic project for the Crow Indian Tribe and the Indian Health Service. Alan was an "announcer," a man of sixty-plus years who speaks publicly for others at giveaways and council meetings, an individual well experienced in his culture. In my desire to learn, I bombarded him with questions, many of which I now realize were rather naive. But he was patient with me—up to a point. After a battery of questions, he held up his hand and pointed to a corrugated-metal building some fifty yards away. It housed Highway Department equipment— trucks and tractors—or so I imagined.

"You see that tin shed?" Alan asked. "It's like my culture. You can sit back here and describe it, but it's not 'til you go inside, listen, feel it, see from the inside looking out, that you really know what it's all about. You've gotta go inside!"

The lessons of the "tin shed" were taken to heart. Twenty years have passed since we sat under that cottonwood. I have come to realize that each of the lessons Alan had so patiently and poignantly shared with me comprise, in fact, points of access as well as primary defining characteristics of a rich and vibrant oral literature, a literature vital to Alan and to so many other Indian peoples. I am convinced that, in the oral literature of the Inland Peoples, we are availed of a

5

The tin shed, Crow Agency, Montana.

wonderful opportunity to enter the "tin shed" to better know the world of the Indian.

The intent of this book is to offer something of the dynamics and structure, something of the vitality and life of the oral literature and storytelling of the Inland Peoples. Our journey through *Stories That Make the World* into the oral literature will follow the path suggested by Alan Old Horn.

See from the inside looking out. Observe what is being said from the perspective of those inside. We must first listen carefully for the meaning within and avoid our own preconceived ideas and biases. What I had imagined within the "tin shed" while standing from afar was not, in fact, what I found once I was inside. The folklorist Alan Dundes has suggested that an interpretation and appreciation of any people's oral literature involves the clarification of the three significant elements of that literature: the text, the texture and the context.[1] The text refers to the meaning embedded within the actual narrative of the story—what is being said, the cultural themes, and the literary characters and motifs represented in the story. The chapter entitled "The Text" focuses on some of the prominent cultural themes and literary motifs embedded within the literature, always attempting to ground them from the perspective of the Indian. We will be introduced to the world of the animal peoples, among them the trickster Coyote, and the creation time in which they live, and to an understanding that humanity shares in a kinship with these peoples and with the natural landscape. Humanity is an active and vital participant in the world.

Feel it. Appreciate the format and style of that which you seek to understand, sensing how it is being said. We would agree that how something is presented is invariably related to what that something means. This is particularly apparent in the telling of an oral literature. For Dundes, the texture refers to how the story is presented—the techniques of the telling and the interactions with the listener's response—as well as the linguistic components and structures of the story. Such components include the particular phonemes and morphemes, the intonation and pitch, pauses, and any "coloration" within the text of the story. Following the discussion of cultural values and literary motifs, we will explore, in the chapter entitled "The Texture," some of the elements of the presentation style and format of the literature, some of the key techniques of storytelling. We will also be introduced to many of the salient characteristics of the oral tradition and the creative power of words. In song and words, in telling the stories, the world is brought forth, made meaningful, and maintained. It is a world participated in. We must consider the critical distinctions between orality and literacy and their implications if we are to begin to appreciate this oral literature.

You've gotta go inside. Engage in and participate with that which you seek to understand. To experience is to know. To stand back from is to remain uninformed. For Dundes, the context refers to whom, when, where and for what purpose the stories are told. A comprehension of the context calls for an understanding of the entire cultural configuration from which the story comes. As we will discover, both the text, the what, and the texture, the how, of oral literature ultimately coalesce in a singular focus, that of participation. As I had first experienced with the Crow stories and, subsequently, with the Coeur d'Alene stories, to know the oral literature is to have been an active participant within it. Included in the chapter entitled, "The Context," is a discussion of the purpose and intent of oral literature as understood by the Indian. And primary to that intent is the integration of humanity into the world—participation.

Throughout this text several stories will be shared that illustrate, and enhance our access to, what can be elusive and abstract cultural themes and literary motifs. The best way to gain an appreciation of the oral literature is, after all, to "go inside" the stories!

The narratives shared by Lawrence Aripa, a Coeur d'Alene; Tom Yellowtail, a Crow; Basil White, a Kootenai; and Mari Watters, a Nez Perce, are derived from actual storytelling performances in which I was involved. Audiotaped recordings of the narratives as told by the storytellers were made and then transcribed into written form. The transcriptions of these stories convey some of their oral qualities: for instance, the storyteller's voiced intonation and emphasis, pause and word phrase patterns, and audience response (when available). One is able to sense the voice of the storyteller in these narratives.

The other stories included here are based on previously written (and published) accounts from other ethnographers. They are derived from story texts originally told in the particular Indian language of the storyteller and then translated into English by the ethnographer. I have recorded here the actual verse translations of those story texts. While lacking much of a sense of their orality, these narratives typically convey their original internal structural dynamics: phrase usage and repetition patterns, for example. Something of the beauty of the native language and the complexity of the literary structure can be glimpsed in these stories.

Taken together, the narratives assembled here, be they Coeur d'Alene, Crow, Kootenai, or Nez Perce, or be they Klikitat, Sanpoil, Wasco, or Wishram, vividly portray the traditional literary motifs and cultural themes found in the oral literature. Each story was selected for a specific purpose—it might be illustrative of the Coyote cycle or of the power of "medicine" or of the techniques used in telling a story. An overview of what is characteristic of as well as essential to the peoples of the region is thus provided.

The various stories presented here, as well as the discussion of their specific literary motifs, cultural themes, and narrative techniques, are drawn from the Indian peoples of the Inland Northwest. It is their perspective that I have attempted to portray in *Stories That Make the World*. That perspective has been greatly influenced by the Crow of Montana and by the Coeur d'Alene of Idaho, along with many other peoples of the region. The Crow, who call themselves Apsáalooke, "children of the large-beaked bird," descend from the once-great buffalo-hunting tradition of the plains area. Today the Crow number some 9,500 individuals, most of whom live on their reservation located in south-central Montana. The Coeur d'Alene are of the plateau region where the peoples once fished the salmon, hunted the deer, gathered the serviceberries, and dug the camas root. The Coeur d'Alene term for the themselves is Schee-chu-umsh, "the ones that were found here."[2] There are over 1,200 Coeur d'Alenes living on their reservation just south of the city and west of the lake that carry their name—Coeur d'Alene. For both the Crow and Coeur d'Alene, their oral literature continues to form an integral and vital part of their contemporary lives.[3]

The plateau region encompasses the Columbia River basin and its various tributaries, extending from the Washington Cascades to the Montana Rockies, from the interior of British Columbia into Oregon. In addition to the Coeur d'Alene, among the peoples of the plateau are the Kalispel, Kootenai, and Nez Perce of Idaho; the Kootenai, Lakes, Lillooet, Okanagan, Shuswap, and Thompson of British Columbia; the Bitterroot Salish (Flathead), Kootenai, and Pend d'Oreille of

Montana; the Cayuse, Klamath, Umatilla, and Wasco of Oregon; and the Columbia, Colville, Klikitat, Okanagan, Palouse, Sahaptin (Yakima), Sanpoil-Nespelem, Spokane, Walla Walla, Wenatchee, and Wishram of Washington. Most of these peoples belong to either the Sahaptin or the Salishian linguistic family. The Crow belong to the Siouan linguistic family and are of the plains region.

Oral Literature, Myths and Tales

Before we begin our journey into the stories, let me take this opportunity to clarify a few key terms and concepts. Our concern is with oral literature, and not oral history. Oral literature and oral history certainly share important qualities in common. Both encompass the verbal arts shared by members of an identifiable social group (ethnic, occupational, familial, or geographic group), and are transmitted orally from person-to-person. The authorship of oral literature and of oral history is often anonymous, seldom easily identifiable with a specific person. The quality of *orality,* be it in oral literature or in oral history, will be shown to be of vital significance in our appreciation of the stories.

But the distinctions are critical. Oral literature is a particular form of literature, involving universal elements of drama, (for example, elaborate plot, rich characters such as heroes and buffoons, unexpected twists and suspense). And embedded within an oral literature are also the revered teachings and sacred truths of a people. How a people define themselves, (for instance, morality and cosmology), how they came to this certain place, (that is, their origin), and what they seek to become, (their destiny) are all revealed in their oral literature. Necessarily, oral literature characteristically refers to what is considered timeless wisdom and is only loosely linked to a specific history.

In contrast, oral history is, above all, history, linked in varying degrees linked to historical events, personalities, and geographic locations, and thus to idiosyn-

Nez Perce salmon feast, ca. 1890. (Courtesy of the Idaho State Historical Society)

cratic, unique events in time and space. Oral history can become an important source of local and family "color," revealing the personality of a place, its time and its people.

In any given cultural setting, oral history and oral literature are typically complementary and often tightly interwoven, perhaps the critical distinction revolves around the type of truth revealed in each form: Oral history is to historical truth as oral literature is to aesthetic and spiritual truth.

There are numerous genres of oral literature—proverbs, riddles, songs, legends, myths, and tales, for example. With regard to Indian oral literature of the Inland Northwest, two particular genres—myths and tales—will be our primary focus.

Mythology comprises the spoken narratives descriptive of the adventures and misadventures of a host of powerful mythic beings. The Thompson Indians call these beings *spela'kl;* the Nez Perce call them *titwatityá·ya."* Among the myth people are Coyote and

Oral Literature, Myths and Tales / 11

Fox, Swallowing Monster and Sweat Lodge, Raccoon and Salmon, Chief Child of the Water and Grizzly Bear. Their adventures transpire in a time "before the coming of human beings." This is the time of transformation in which the world, its animals, plants, landforms, its customs and ways of relating, and, finally, its human peoples are all brought into being. For instance, it is Coyote who travels up the Columbia River, freeing the fish from the Swallow Sisters and establishing the importance of the Sweat Bath. In the collective actions of the myth people, every ridge and gully, every creek and pond, every plant and animal, every human custom is rendered meaningful and spiritually potent. The Coeur d'Alene call the narratives about the myth people, *me-y-mi-ym q̓esp schint,* roughly translated "he/she is going to tell stories about the time before the human beings."

While a majority of mythic beings are given the names of animals, as Archie Phinney, a Nez Perce, once stated, there is "no clear picture" of the physical image of the myth people "offered or needed."[4] The myth people are appropriately and simply referred to as "persons." While they possess the animal qualities venerated by the Indian—Coyote as cunning or foolish and Wolf as wildly aggressive and dangerous— they are also portrayed with human motivations— compassion and bravery, humor and folly, greed and vengeance. In addition, the myth people consistently demonstrate what in the Coeur d'Alene language is termed *súumesh,* and in Apsáalooke (Crow), *baaxpée,* "spiritual power." The trickster Coyote best illustrates this power, from an ability to transform himself into a piece of driftwood to the slaying of monsters to being brought back to life from the dead (with the help of Fox or Mrs. Mole). The myth people are thus inclusive of a full range of expression and ability as well as physical imagery, interweaving the qualities of animal-plant-object with those of humans and deities.[5]

It should be stressed that the term *myth,* as applied to Indian mythology, refers to that which is considered a "deeply true story." Myth is not to be understood here as fable, fiction, or illusion. As Henry SiJohn, a Coeur d'Alene elder, has said, "We survive by our oral traditions, which are our basic truths, our basic facts, handed down from our elders. They are the basis for our songs, our vision quests, our sharing."

The "truth" of a myth is expressed metaphorically and anagogically as opposed to empirically and literally. Hence, myth is not bound to a history as a factual event occurring in chronological time. It is not oral history. It is not even a past event. Myth is considered timeless, integrating time and space into a singular phenomenon, human with animal and landscape with the creation era. Myth is thus imbued with tremendous aesthetic and spiritual significance.

Having completed his travels up the Columbia, transforming the land and bringing forth the animal, the plant, and, finally, the human peoples, Coyote himself enters that landscape—as do all the other myth people. With the coming of human peoples, the myth people take on the particular forms and characteristics associated with grizzly bear, wolf, elk, salmon, eagle, frog, mouse, becoming those beings—though Coyote, as himself, may on occasion still be encountered, as he is in the Coeur d'Alene story "Coyote and the White Man." In fact, the Pend d'Oreille have accounts of Coyote visiting Catholic missionaries! Regardless of Coyote's antics, the special meanings and spiritual powers of the myth people are now vested throughout the newly transformed world.

If myths relate the story of transformation and preparation, tales recount the time *after* the coming of the human peoples. Called *me-y-mi-ymⱡu schint*[6] by the Coeur d'Alene, meaning "he/she is going to tell stories about the human beings," and *txa'nat* by the Klikitat, literally meaning "happenings or customs," tales are narratives descriptive of the actions of humans. Tales are not, however, oral histories. While they may refer to specific historical figures, tales reverberate with the dominant literary and archetypical characters and patterns of the cultural tradition of which they are a part. The Coeur d'Alene stories of Cosechin and Four Smokes and the Crow stories of Burnt Face, Little Head and Wise Man are all examples of tales. Even in these instances, each of which involves an identifiable or presumed historical personage, the overall narrative structure embodies pervasive archetypal qualities—trickster or orphan quest literary motifs, for example.

Like myths, tales are invariably linked with the surrounding landscape, referring to this river or that mountain valley. The land is a richly endowed with mythic meanings and references. It is a landscape spiritually endowed. It may be a bear, an elk, or a mouse that is seen on a hillside, but it is the spirit of Bear, Elk, or Mouse embodied in that animal that comes to a human as a guardian spirit. It may even be the Little People, known by the Crow as the *awakkulé,* who "pay you a visit." Refer to Tom Yellowtail's account of Burnt Face and his story, "The Little People," for a glimpse of the *awakkulé.* Tales often convey a story involving human peoples seeking to acquire that which the myth people inherently exhibit—*súumesh.* In a vision quest, an individual seeks to establish a relationship with a guardian spirit, a *titwatityá·ya*—Bear, Wolf, or Eagle.

And, like myths, tales illustrate a full range of human characteristics and motivations, from compassion to vengeance, from generosity to greed, from bravery to foolishness. The Crow stories "Burnt Face" and "The Couple Befriended by the Moon" are such tales. Both involve the theme of rising from poverty and destitution through adoption by a guardian spirit to triumph over once-formidable obstacles.

The world of myth necessarily precedes, yet continues to reverberate throughout, the world of tales. The myth people still travel the landscape, a mythic landscape.

I

FOUR SMOKES
Lawrence Aripa, Coeur d'Alene[7]

Our people . . were . . . always . . around the lake . .
　　as far back as anybody can tell.
We've always lived around the lake,
　　the Coeur d'Alene Lake.
And . . then . . in the seventeen hundreds sometime . . the horse was
introduced,
　　and we were able to go . . go farther then we ever did before.
And so . . a lot of the people traveled,
　　and they went to very far distances.
And so our people used to join with the Kalispels,
　　and the Flatheads,
　　　　and the . . Spokanes,
　　　　　　and even the Nez Perce.
And they would go . . all the way into South Dakota
　　or eastern Montana,
　　　　and hunt the *buffalo* . . .

And so . . when you think about it . . you think,
　　"Well, *why* did they have to go *that far* just for *buffalo*? . .
　　　　when they have elk,
　　　　　　and deer,
　　　　　　　　bear,
　　　　all over here.
　　Why would they go that far just for the *buffalo*?"
Well . . there . . was *other things* that they learned from those trips.
The whole family would go,
　　and one man would be chosen
　　　　and his family would go with him.
And they'd always used to say . . that,
　　"The children would *leave* . . . as children,
　　　　but they'd come back . . as grown ups,"
　　　　　　because they'd *learn so much* . . on these trips.
They would learn about different . . Indians,
　　about different *foods* they'd pick up along the way,

and they'd learn . . all kinds of things.
In fact they . . even received *names* . . by going on these trips . . .

One of my ancestors . . was a boy about . . *thirteen years old,*
    but he was *very large,*
        he was almost six feet ta-a-ll,
            just about the size of a . . of a man.
And so they were going,
    and it was the practice that when they got close to the buffalo,
        the warriors and the hunters . . would go out and look for the
        buffalo,
            and the women and children and the old people
            would stay . . in camp.
They were the ones that would . . cut up the meat and everything,
    prepare it once it . . was brought in.
And so . . he had to stay with the old people and the children,
    and the women . . .

And a . . after the hunters left . . it happened that there was a *Crow war
party* that came . . upon them,
    and they were *high on* the hill.
And they looked down,
    and . . they thought to themselves.,
        "This is going to be easy.
            All there is is women and children."
And they *used to take* our children especially for slaves.
And they would raise them as slaves in their camps.
And so . . the Crows were . . one of our natural enemies,
    because we didn't speak their language,
        and because *actually* we were invading . . their territory
            their *hunting* grounds.
So . . there was always a fight
    and they'd always be glad to try to get some . . *captives.*

And so . . . in the meantime . . inside the camp one of the old men . . called the
boy,
    and he says,
        "You know you're about the same size . . as a *grown man,*
            and from a distance they will think you *are* a man."
So he takes him to the edge of the *camp.*

And in the meantime . . the warriors up on the hill . . are taking their time,
    they says,
        "We don't have to worry,
            we don't have to hurry,
                we can just go down
                    and just pick them up without any problem. ". .

And so the old man told the boy,
    he says,
        "Out there . . about a hundred yards . . there was a rock."
And he says . .
        "You take this stick
            and pretend like it's a bow and arrow,
                or maybe like a rifle." . . .
And he says,
        "And *you* make a *war cry*,
            and you head for that rock,
                and *run . . as fast* as you can,
                    and just go . . zigzag all the way."
And so the boy says
    "Alright!"

So just as . . the Crows were goin' . . head down the hill,
    the boy jumps out,
        and he yells
            he gives *a big war whoop.*
And when . . he does that they look,
    and then the boy comes running out waving . . the stick,
        and they must of thought it was a rifle.
So then he started to run.
And then they said,
    "There is only one man . . in the camp so we can kill him."
And they watched him as he ran.
And they all shot . . .
And when they shot with their . . muskets the smoke went up in the air,
    and . . they missed . . .
And he ran as *hard* as he could,
    he kept thinking,
        "I'm going to die,
            I'm going to die." (in a rapid, scared voice)

But he didn't . .
He got behind the rock,
    and he was tired,
        and he laid there,
            and he says . . .
                "I'm not hit, . . .
                    they didn't even touch me!" . . (in an amazed
                    voice)

So he looks out,
    and there's a brush about *another hundred* yards.
And so he waits
    and he . . thinks that it would be enough time for them to
    reload.
And then he takes off running
Again he gives the war whoop,
    the war cry,
        and he *runs again.*
Again just as fast as he can.
And again they fire at him.
And again they miss.

And again he *still can't* believe it.
    "All those warriors,
        they're suppose to be . . expert shots.
            They're suppose to be the best in the . . in the country,
                and they haven't even touched me!" . .
And so he says,
    "Well, I'll go back to the *rock* then."
In the meantime the camp had got their things together
    and they were taking off . . down in the gully.
        They were . . running away,
            they were *moving then.*

And then the Crow then concentrated . . on the boy.
They says,
    "We're going to kill him." . .
So when he . . run back from the bush
    and went back to the rock *again,*

they did the same thing,
  they fired.

And by that time,
  the Indians, of course, were superstitious,
   at that time,
  and they also believed in *special powers.*
A man . . or a person could have special powers where *he couldn't* be hurt.
And so . . the third time . . they started to . . *think about* it.
And so,
  "We can . . shoot at this man . . all day,
   and we can't hit him because he has special powers.
  Nobody can kill this man."

And so . . the *fourth time* when he run from the rock back to the original
place, . .
  they said,
   "He *has* . . special powers! (deliberate voice)
    And if he wants to . . all he has to do is come
     and he'd kill *all of us.*"
  They said,
   "We'd just better leave him *alone!*"
So then they left.

And when they left . . the hunters came back,
  and they . . caught up to the camp.
And then . . . the old man told the story about the boy.
And so . . they start . . telling the story,
  retelling it,
   and,
    "*Oh*, that was a *great thing* that boy did.
     He was a *hero.*
      And he was a *special boy.*"
And so . . that evening. . . . one of them . . mentioned,
  he says,
   "You know . . . he does not have *a name!*
    He is thirteen years old
     but he has never been out . . on his quest
      he has never found an *animal* to imitate,
       a súumesh,

and so he has never *found one* yet.
So this is an opportunity to give him a name." . .
So that night all of the tribes had a council,
the Spokanes. .
the . . Nez Perce. .
Kalispels,
all the headmen got together with the medicine . . people,
and then they discussed it.
So they met for about an hour . .
And the boy . . he didn't know what was going on,
he didn't know *what* they were going to do
and so he was *very anxious.*
And then all of a sudden they came out of . . the main tipi.
They came out
and one of . . the old . . medicine men . . . asked . . to make an
announcement.
"Each time that the Crow would . . . fire blue smoke would come
up from their . . muskets,
and it would go up in a *cloud* like.
And so that happened . . *four times.*
There were *four smokes!*"
And so that's how he got the name,
Moos-sim-mot. . .[8]

Orality in a Literate Society

Ironically, accessing this particular introduction to an oral-based literature presupposes a thorough competency in literacy. After all, you must read from the pages of this book that which was intended to be heard spoken by a storyteller. Indeed, as I will attempt to demonstrate, there are fundamental distinctions between orality and literacy. Questions naturally arise: How should a literature based in oral tradition and in the act of storytelling be conveyed in writing to a literacy-based audience, rendering that literature accessible without compromising its unique oral nuances? If we are to utilize a written format, as I have done here, how do we best express a literature akin to an event, a literature based in the dynamics of orality?[9]

The resolution of this dilemma is at best only partial.

Nevertheless, I have endeavored in this book to present stories in a format that conveys some semblance of their oral dimensions. In the printed texts I have attempted to replicate not only the actual phrasing of the narrative but also much of the pacing and rhythm and the structural patterning of that phrasing. When possible, I have transcribed the exact speech patterns of the storyteller—dramatic rhythms and pauses, intentional repetitions, stress placed on certain phrases, as well as hand gestures and facial expressions. And, when they were available, the written text also includes listener interactions and responses to the unfolding story. (In those narrative transcriptions from recordings, you will also glimpse examples of contemporary "Indian English".)

The various conventions that guided the formatting of all the story texts that appear here include identification and marking of verses, scenes, and word intonation and stress. As a result, the stories resemble poetry more than prose. This is as it should be, for in poetry the voice of the teller is more clearly represented. I hope that through this manner of presentation appreciation of oral literature will be enhanced, that authentic oral literature will be made accessible to a wide audience, and that the reader will indeed *participate* in the stories.

Verses designate word phrases—or more precisely, "morpheme clusters"— within the narrative. Each verse is formatted as a line in the text and is typically delineated by a comma or a period. During the actual storytelling, each verse is usually set off by an introductory phrase such as "It is said" or "He said"; or, as in the Coeur d'Alene, Crow, and Nez Perce stories, by a coordinating conjunction such as "and;" or by a pause. The length of the pauses will vary with each storyteller, from a half a second or so to as many as three seconds. Commas indicate very brief pauses, while periods mark longer pauses. Extended pauses also appear within a verse, or may separate verses, and are indicated by a series of dot ellipses. These pauses are often added by the storyteller for dramatic effect. We

Reeds and waves,
Lake Coeur d'Alene,
Idaho.

will see in the storytelling style of both Tom Yellowtail
and Basil White a very slow and deliberate pacing, with
frequent use of extended pauses.

Scenes are groupings of actions related to a given
locale and specific characters; scenes are set off here
by double spacing. Scenes reflect the structural patterns within the narrative and not necessarily, as with
verses, marked by any overt gestures or pauses by the
storyteller. There are instances, as in the Nez Perce story,
as told by Mari Watters, where separate scenes are ac-
tually linked, voiced as closely associated verses. (When
relying upon written narrative accounts, one should
be aware that repetitive phrases are sometimes deleted
by the editor and that the text itself may be a "free
translation" of the original Indian language. Elements
of the original verse and scene integrity are sometimes
thereby lost.)

Word *intonation* and *stress* (voiced inflection of morphemes) are marked here by *italicizing* the stressed words.
Intonational colorings can be found in the stories shared
by Aripa, Watters, White, and Yellowtail. As there is
some degree of variation in the inflection patterns used
by these storytellers, the stress markings given here
are only approximate indicators of the actual emphasis
placed on morphemes.

Storyteller *gestures* and listener *responses*—hand and

Bitterroot River near Missoula, Montana.

facial expressions, linguistic and physical reactions, including smiles, laughter, tears, and comments—are described within parentheses. Audience responses are found especially in the Coeur d'Alene stories. As we will discover, a story is told only as long as there are overt listener responses and participation.

Some of the language used in previously published texts may be rather dated. For example, Edward Sapir's *Wishram Texts* was originally published in 1909. In order to render the stories more accessible and the phrasing within the texts consistent, I have generally substituted more commonly used expressions for archaic English terms—for example, *stayed* for *staid*—and, on occasion, I have slightly altered the phrasing within a given verse. However, I have made a conscious effort to maintain the verse patterns and the meanings conveyed in the original transcription.

A final consideration. In order to heighten a sense of the oral nuance in the stories, I would suggest that you first access the narratives in *Stories That Make the World* through the voice of someone else. Have a friend read these stories aloud to you. He or she should vary the duration of the pauses as indicated by commas and periods, and place stress on the phrases given in italicized type. Some of the rhythm, the pacing, and the coloration within the stories can be better appreciated as you hear a particular phrase emphasized and experience the silence of an extended pause. As a result, the story will become a little more like an *event.* It is a literature meant to be heard, performed in the company of others.

In short, a literal translation of the literature of another culture is difficult at best. This is particularly evident in working with oral texts. While I have identified the original sources and have tried to maintain their cultural and literary integrity, the presentations of the stories included in this book are not the same as their telling by an elder. Absent are certain qualities of orality, of the way they were told aloud, and often of specific phrasings and verse structures. The stories shared here are thus a retelling, mediating the need to render accessible to a wide audience authentic oral narratives. While the letter of the narratives may not be conveyed here, I hope that something of the spirit is.

It may be gleaned from these introductory comments and from the stories to come that the oral literature of the American Indian represents a very distinct genre from that of the other literatures with which you may be familiar. To truly appreciate this literature, we must leave behind what we imagined to be in the "tin shed" in order to begin to know what is truly to be found within.

I

THE COUPLE BEFRIENDED
BY THE MOON
YOUNG CRANE, CROW[10]

Over there,
    the Crow people are coming.
They are walking towards the mountains.
It's a big camp.

A man,
    who does not see well,
        has a wife.

They have only one horse;
    their lodge is small,
        packed on one side of the horse;
    they have little meat,
        packed on one side of the horse.
With a root digger,
    the woman gathers plant foods.
They are on one side of the camp;
    a hunter kills plenty of game animals;
    the couple takes some of it.

The people are camped there;
    the couple are camped on the outside of the encampment.
They are very poor;
    they follow the tracks of the people when they travel.
The woman lets her husband hold her horse;
    she goes out digging roots.

The Moon comes,
    from where the wife does not know.
The Moon befriends the wife.
This Moon is a woman;
    she wears an elk-tooth dress.
From where the Moon comes the wife does not know;
    the Moon has a big blue-handled knife.
From where the Moon comes the wife does not know.

Then the wife comes there,
    to one side of the road.
Then Moon comes,
    to one side of the road.
"Daughter,
    look for someone to assist you;
        your husband is nearly blind," the Moon says.

The people are camped there;
    the couple are camped on the outside of the encampment.
There is plenty of meat;
    the people stay for some time.
"We are poor;

The Couple Befriended by the Moon / 25

Rock Valley College - ERC

I have been told to look for someone to assist us;
   over there at the Musselshell River there are horses for you,"
the wife says.
"A roan,
   a big-bellied mare are there," she says.

The Hidatsa are camped there.
Those who do not have guns, powder, tobacco, horses,
   they traded for these things.
Then they travel on,
   towards the mountains.

The wife has some powdered turnips.
"Make some pudding from the turnips," the husband says.
"Call to our lodge,
   four very brave young men," he says.
The wife calls in the four young men.
She gives them some pudding;
   they eat.

The husband is there,
   with the four young men.
"Have your moccasins made," he says.
"My horses are at the Musselshell River;
   let us go there," he says.
The wife smokes the pipe with the men.

The four young men go out from the lodge.
"When you have gone out,
   have moccasins made," the couple say.
These four young men go out from the lodge,
   they meet,
      they speak with one another.

Two of young men are friends;
   the other two are also friends.
"Well,
   what are we going to do about this offer?" one young man says.
"If he really has good medicine,

Crow horses.

he would not be a poor man," the first young men say.
"We will go with him," the other two young men say.

The wife cuts up her lodge cover;
      she makes moccasins from it.
"When you go tonight,
      your moccasins will be ready," she says.
The wife makes a padded saddle for her husband.
"When you bring in your horses,
      ride on this saddle," she says.
The Moon had given the wife an hourglass-shaped medicine bag.
They tie the bag inside their lodge.

When it gets dark,
      two young men come;
            "We have come," they say.
The other two young men had doubted the man;
      they do not come.
"We have come," they say.
"Wait for me outside the lodge;
      I am getting ready," the husband says.
Then the husband comes outside.

Then the wife takes the medicine bag;
      she goes outside with her husband.
The husband packs the padded saddle;

he is ready.
The wife sings a glad song.
A fine scouting song she sings.
"Go that way;
    the roan is at the Musselshell River," she says.

When it gets dark,
    then the three men go.
At the Yellowstone River,
    the three men kill a very fat buffalo.
The three men build a fire;
    the meat is cooked;
        the three men pack the meat;
            they will eat of this meat.
From now on,
    the three men do not build a fire.

"Here is the Musselshell River," the three men say.
"Now,
    go.
        I will stay here," the husband says.
"In the mountain valley there is a herd of horses;
    bring them to me," he says.

"Look for the roan," the husband says.
The young men search for the roan;
    it is among the herd of horses.
They capture the roan;
    they drive it back.
They take it to the poor man.

"Here is the roan,
    take it," they say.
They give it to him.
The man puts the padded saddle on the roan;
    he rides the roan.

"Look for the big-bellied mare," the husband says.
The young men search for the mare;
    it is among the herd of horses.

Buffalo in Montana.

They capture the mare;
    they drive it back to the man.
The man puts a rope on the mare;
    he leads the mare.

"Let the horses come," the husband says.
The young men drive the horses behind the man.
They come to Bull Hill;
    there they swim with their horses across Pryor Creek.

"Those with medicine will find what they seek;
    those without medicine will come last," they say.

They bring in to the camp eighty horses;
    the two young men have ten horses each;
        this man has sixty horses.
"They have come with horses," the people say.
"That man really has medicine," they say.
All three men have geldings.

When they get to the edge of the camp,
    this man cuts out his sixty horses he brought.
When he comes with horses,
    they buy a very large lodge;
        they furnish the lodge with the horses brought;
            now they have something.

Pryor Creek south of
Billings, Montana.

The young men are in the couple's lodge;
        praise songs are sung;
            in their own lodge,
                praise songs are sung.
"With medicine I will find what I seek;
        four times I will find what I seek," says one young man.
"With medicine I will find what I seek;
        four times I will find what I seek," says the other young man.

"Look for someone to assist you,
        that is what the Moon said," the wife says.
"These two young men who took pity on us,

they really have medicine," she says.
"Those two young men who insulted us,
    they do not have medicine," she says.
"When you go on a horse raid,
    send those two young men away,
        send them home," she says.

The two young men who pitied the couple go on a horse raid;
    they would bring many horses;
        they would take many coups;
            they are very good.
A group of young men go on a horse raid;
    when those who insulted the couple go,
        they would be sent away by themselves;
            now they cry.

That is the end.

The Storytellers

Before we go any further into the stories, let me briefly introduce two of our storytellers—Lawrence Aripa and Tom Yellowtail—and describe my relationship with each man.

Lawrence Aripa is a Coeur d'Alene. He was born on March 26, 1926, on the Coeur d'Alene Reservation in Idaho. His family had originally lived "in the St. Joe river area." As with other heads of Coeur d'Alene families, his great-grandfather, Shet-sin, had been given a Christian name, Albert, after Saint Albert, by the local priests. But the name, when spoken in Coeur d'Alene, was "difficult to pronounce by us Indians," and over time "Albert" became "A-rap-a" and then "A-rip-a."

As a very young child, Lawrence remembers listening to the stories of his great-grandmothers, Mattie Garry and Susan Aripa. Mattie was a Spokane, and though blind, "she could weave beautiful braid rugs!" Lawrence loved to hear her stories, especially about how she had been at the Battle of Steptoe. In May of 1858 a U.S. Army colonel by the name of Steptoe attempted to march his troops north to Fort Colville

Lawrence Aripa,
June 1993.

through Coeur d'Alene territory. Some fifty Nez Perce scouts accompanying the troops had "bragged that the army was going to beat us and take our lands," Mattie Garry told her great-grandson. But at the Battle of Steptoe, the Coeur d'Alenes, in alliance with the Spokanes and the Palouse, "drove the army out," at least temporarily. When Mattie died in 1937, she was well over a hundred years of age. Susan Aripa, Lawrence's other great-grandmother, was Coeur d'Alene and almost a hundred years old when she died in 1931.

In the house in which they all lived when Lawrence was growing up, the grandmothers didn't get along very well—Susan was Catholic and Mattie was Protestant—and each woman had "her own corner." Lawrence remembers going from one corner to the other, asking for and being told stories, stories that "always had a lesson to teach me." The stories of Mattie Garry continued until Lawrence, in 1933, went to the Jesuit-run DeSmet boarding school located on the reservation. There he was not allowed to speak his native language, and he soon lost touch with his great-grandmother Mattie.

Besides storytelling, drawing has always been an important part of Lawrence's life. Henry, his older brother, remembers how, as a child, Lawrence used to "draw cows and horses on the walls" of his room. After serving in the navy during World War II, Lawrence worked at the Navy Supply Depot in Spokane, Washington. While working at the depot, he illustrated an operations and safety manual with cartoon characters he had created. In 1972 and 1973, he taught at the Indian Art Institute in Santa Fe, and for the next eighteen years he owned and operated his own art gallery, the Indian Art Shop, located on the reservation in Idaho. During those years, he would attend local powwows, doing charcoal portraits of the people who visited his booth. Lawrence also designed the Coeur d'Alene tribal seal and one side of the Idaho state centennial coin. For the last twelve years, he has served on the Coeur d'Alene tribal council and has been active in his Catholic faith, attending the Sacred Heart Mission at DeSmet. (Catholicism was brought to the Coeur d'Alenes by Father DeSmet and "the Black Robes" in 1842.)

I have known and worked with Lawrence since 1990. We have been involved in local projects that have brought the stories of the Coeur d'Alene to north Idaho communities and schools. He is a gifted storyteller, always able to relate his stories to young and old, to Indian and non-Indian. While fluent in Coeur d'Alene—"though sometimes I get my words confused with Spokane"—Lawrence more frequently tells his stories in English. A great translator of the "old stories," he has become a fine "ambassador of the Indian ways." I've come to appreciate his warm smile, his kindness toward others and his tremendous joy in storytelling. His stories vitalize both those listening and himself.

The six stories Lawrence has shared in *Stories That*

Make the World are stories I have heard him tell numerous times. He particularly delights in telling "Four Smokes" whenever he knows I am in the audience, for he knows of my close association with the Crows. It is an account of the Coeur d'Alene "counting coups" on the Crows, with whom they historically "didn't get along." The texts for five of the narratives included here were derived from recordings made during a series of well-attended public presentations in communities throughout north Idaho in the spring of 1991. Non-Indians made up the majority of those in the audience.[11] The sixth story, "Coyote and the Woman," was added by Lawrence as "a good one to finish off" the other narratives he had shared. When asked to tell stories about the Coeur d'Alene people, these six are primary among those Lawrence delights in telling. After I had transcribed his stories, Lawrence "read them over" for any comments or corrections. In one instance—"Coyote and the White Man"—he had me add several verses he had forgotten in the original telling. "There are so many Coyote stories," he explained, "that sometimes I leave something out."

Thomas Yellowtail was born just south of Lodge Grass on the Crow Reservation of Montana on March 7, 1903.[12] His Indian name was Medicine Rock Chief, given him by Medicine Crow, the famous warrior and chief born around 1848. Tom also received the name *Dashbiiláa,* Fire Heart. It was this name that you would hear, spoken in Apsáalooke, calling him to the center pole of the Sun Dance lodge to "doctor" someone. Tom's father was Yellowtail, of the Big Lodge clan, born around 1855. The name *Yellowtail,* is in probable reference to the ferruginous "yellowtail" hawk. Tom's mother was Lizzie Chienne, of the Whistling Water clan, born in 1864. Tom's father passed on in 1927 and his mother, "living over a hundred years," passed on in 1969. In 1929 Tom married Susie Walking Bear; it was the beginning of a very close and "wonderful partnership." In 1970 at the All-American Indian Days in Sheridan, Wyoming, Tom and Susie were together honored as the Outstanding American Indian of the Year. On Christmas Day 1981 Susie passed on. Almost twelve years later, on November 24, 1993, Tom Yellowtail followed her "to the other side camp."

Tom was a deeply spiritual man, an *akbaalía,* "one who doctors." I was first introduced to him at a Sun Dance he was "running" near Pryor, Montana. It was his responsibility to coordinate the entire three-day ceremony of fasting, prayer, and doctoring for the over 100 men and women participants. Tom had "danced" in over fifty Sun Dances. In 1984 Tom "retired" as an active "Sun Dance medicine man," passing many of his "medicines" on to John Pretty on Top. Nevertheless, as an *akbaalía,* Tom continued to provide "doctoring" for all those who were in need of his help. In fact, he was very active up to the end of his life, conducting "bundle openings" and "prayer meetings." During the July 1993 Sun Dance sponsored by Alvin Howe and Rob Moran, Tom, then ninety years old, was at the center pole "doctoring." That fall, he traveled to Colorado, Indiana, and Illinois, offering prayers and "doctoring." He attended the Parliament of the World's Religions in Chicago, where he offered prayers for world peace with the Dalai Lama of Tibet and other spiritual leaders. In November, Tom again answered the call, and was on the Warm Springs Reservation, Oregon, "helping those in trouble." In addition to the "Sun Dance Religion," Tom was also an active member of the Lodge Grass First Crow Indian Baptist Church. For Tom, all religions were connected "like the separate spokes of a wagon wheel," and led to the same "hub," the Creator. The different religions were " just different ways of praying," he said.

The care Tom showed those in need was also shown in one of his great passions, gardening. As soon as I arrived at his cabin in Wyola, Montana, for a visit in June of 1993, the first thing Tom wanted to show me was his garden. We walked out to the plot, an eighth of an acre in size. As we walked down each row, Tom identified each plant for me and inspected it as if it

Tom Yellowtail, 1977.

were a child to be nurtured. Almost every year since 1929, when he had acquired this land, Tom had put in his garden with the help of his wife, Susie, and with each harvest, beets, potatoes, carrots, corn, and radishes "as big as apples" were shared with his family and friends.

As with a majority of Crows, Tom was as fluent in Apsáalooke as he was in English. While I myself had begun to learn Apsáalooke, though far from fluent, the stories Tom shared with me and his wonderful conversations were in English. Even so, Tom's speech patterns retained the same deliberate, repetitive, comprehensive qualities as his Apsáalooke. Having acquired a reputation for "extremely long, though beautifully spoken prayers," there were some who are leery of taking a sweat bath with him. "He'd pour a hot, long sweat!" And Tom would say, "I try to include everyone in my prayers." One can sense some of this Apsáalooke-to-English continuity in the stories Tom has included here.

There is a word in Apsáalooke that for me has best come to express who Tom Yellowtail was. That word is *díakaashe,* literally meaning "he/she is really doing it" and generally translated by the Crow as "sincerity." I know of no other human being who better exemplified this most cherished Crow quality. Tom had a reputation for having "never gotten angry at another person"—or even of having spoken badly of anyone—for honesty, for compassion, for his kind and gentle ways, and for always assisting those in need. These qualities were publicly acknowledged in January of 1993 when Tom was honored for his contribution to the peoples of Montana as the recipient of the Governor's Award for Traditional Arts. Tom's "sincerity" is expressed in the care to which he had shared his stories, faithful and honest to their traditions and to his "medicine fathers."

I first got to know Tom Yellowtail in 1974, when I began working with the Crows on a series of applied ethnographic projects. Soon after, I was calling him "Grandpa." He and Susie had took me in as a "grandson," and during a "bundle opening," Tom bestowed on me the Indian name, *Maakuuxshiichiilish,* "Seeking to Help Others." *Dashbiiláa* has been my guide every time I have "gone in and used the whistle" as a participant in the Sun Dance. "Grandpa" was my most important teacher.

While I heard Tom tell the four stories included here many times over the years, the text for them was obtained in June of 1993, through a recording made at his cabin in Wyola. Those listening with me that evening included Tom's grandson, David, and three of Tom's great-grandchildren. Following their transcription, I had Tom review the stories for his comments and corrections. At the conclusion of his telling of these four "little short stories," as he called them, Tom said, "If all these great stories were told, . . . great stories will come!"

I

The Text

"Seeing from the Inside Looking Out"

*I*n *myths and tales* are reflected the quintessential literary motifs and cultural themes that define and give meaning to the world. The adventures of the myth people tell of overwhelming challenges, of desertion and deception, of contests for power, of foolishness, of revenge, of quests and triumphs, of self-sacrifice and compassion. In these adventures, the myth people such as Coyote and Fox create and subsequently transform the land—rivers are channeled and mountains built, animal and plant peoples are given their particular characteristics, customs are established that govern the relations among all peoples, and the human peoples are brought forth into this world. Monsters and giants that had once roamed this land are slain by the myth people. The world and virtually every detail of its landscape, from the rush of a waterfall or a stream to the towering of a rock outcropping or mountain ridge, from the flight of an eagle or a chickadee to the howl of a coyote or squeak of a mouse, from the thunder of a spring storm to the setting of the sun—all is recounted in the stories. It is a landscape mythically endowed. As the Bitterroot Salish poet and playwright Vic Charlo once told me, "The stories define us. When the story ended, the elder would say, And this is true, pointing to that hill where the heart of the Monster is. And you look and see, see the story; we are linked. It's a matter of just claiming that linkage."

A closer look at the oral literature reveals attitudes

and values toward family and kinship, toward nature and spirit, toward life and death, toward industry and pleasure. The oral literature conveys the conventional wisdom as well as the spontaneous humor of a people. In the stories, fundamental cultural themes of time and space, of causation and being are reaffirmed. What is meaningful in this world is made known through the telling of the stories. Let us "see from the inside looking out."

Cultural Themes

Embedded within the narratives are a rich assortment of cultural themes. For introductory purposes, let me isolate five fundamental themes, each of which significantly defines the world of the Inland Peoples. These cultural themes are kinship, equality, meaning, life-force, and spiritual transcendence. Taken together, these five themes espouse the notion of human beings as unequivocally linked and as vital participants in the world. It is certainly acknowledged that these five cultural themes do not exhaust the themes that pervade the literature.[1] But they will serve us well as points of entry.

Reflected in the worldview expressed in this oral literature is the theme of *kinship*, a *connectedness* throughout the world. All components—animal, plant, human, physical, spirit—while overtly differentiated, are linked as a single indivisible whole. There are no autonomous segments, separate from the whole. We can see this notion clearly illustrated in the concept of *person*. Kinship with the animal, plant, and mythic beings is extended, acknowledging each as a person, part of a web of interconnected relationships. Among the Coeur d'Alene the term *chnis-teem-ilqwes* refers to this understanding. *Chnis-teem-ilqwes* means "I am part of all," having an all-inclusive kinship with the animals and plants, with the earth and sky, as well as with humans. In "Seal Boy," a Wasco story, a lost boy is taken in by the Seals, cared for and raised as one of their own. Upon being "caught," he tells how the seals are "people just like humans," with "names." The children of the Eagle, whom Burnt Face saves from the Long Otter, are his "brother and sister." It is Coyote who makes the human peoples from the flesh of one of the myth people, Swallowing Monster. Any distinctions between human, animal, and mythic people are minimal. We are reminded that the greatest punitive action that can be brought to bear for a misdeed is not seizure of property nor even corporal punishment. It is the threat of ostracism, of being cut off from one's ties. All phenomena are intrinsically interconnected.

Within this web of kinship relationships, the members share in an *equality* with one another, in what the Coeur d'Alene term *unshat-qn*. While a plant can be overtly distinguished from an animal and from a human by its particular physical form and attributes, each has ultimate equality with the others. Kinship, rather than class distinction, predominates. No one kinsperson should be subordinate to another. There are no hierarchical relationships. As Cliff SiJohn was explaining the meaning of *unshat-qn* to me, he referred to its expression in Indian sign language. To give the sign for *unshat-qn,* you move your hand, palm down, out from your eyes toward the "person" you are addressing, be it "a human or an animal." All eyes are at the same level! While on a vision quest, the smallest of creatures, the ant, is to be respected, for it may offer you a gift. A seal can become a "parent" to a human boy. All phenomena—plant, animal, rock, and human—are inherently equal with the others.

Equality is often conveyed in terms of the *respect* to be shown all life forms, termed *pute-nts* by the Coeur d'Alene. If camas root is to be dug or bark taken from a birch or cedar tree to fashion a basket, "permission" must first be sought. A prayer is offered. Before the huge cottonwood tree is cut down to become the center pole in the Sun Dance lodge, "permission" is requested in prayer. If a hunter is to successfully track a deer, respect must be given, respect often shown in terms of "not taking too much," "using all that is taken," or "never boasting about the hunt." When such respect is shown, the deer, in reciprocity may offer itself up to the hunter. The story "Elk and the Young Man" vividly illustrates what can occur when respect is withheld. As illustrated in the Burnt Face narrative, if a guardian spirit is to come, to instruct, and to offer power, the gifts of fasting and of self-sacrifice must be given. Each of the peoples gives to the others in respect.

The world abounds with *meaning*. It offers archetypes to live by, what the Coeur d'Alene call, *mi-yp,* "teachings from all things." As ordained by Sweat Lodge and by Coyote, the various animal peoples are to instruct the human peoples in how best to live in this land. Seeing an eagle while you are on a long journey is not just sighting a large diurnal bird of prey, it may also signify that you will be watched over and will reach your destination safely; the Bird has revealed itself to you. For Burnt Face, what is revealed by the Eagle is indeed a great gift. The world is not void of meaning; it offers messages and lessons, rich in patterns and models—if one is attentive.

Not only does the world abound in meaning, it also radiates a *life force*. This is the power of life, that which animates all things—plant, animal, human, even feather and rock. This is the power exhibited in the actions of the myth people, the bringing forth of the world we now travel. This is the power sought in a vision quest and the power directed onto a patient during the healing ceremony. This is the power that transforms what Burnt Face has "hated" and brings Coyote back to life, when Fox jumps over him. This is what is termed in the Coeur d'Alene language, *súu-mesh,* and in Crow, *baaxpée,* spiritual power. The world is neither dead nor inanimate but provides meaning and power throughout all phenomena.

While not denying a world of overt and material forms, the Inland Peoples know of a reality beyond this, the world of *spiritual transcendence*. This is the world, "from horizon to horizon," that the Coeur d'Alene call *Snq-hepi-wes.* The term roughly means "where the spirit lives," inclusive of all things—animal, plant, rock, water, and sky as well as the human self. This is the dwelling place of the souls of all life forms and of the myth people and guardian spirits. This is the realm from which a vision emanates and the power to cure emerges. This is the world in which Burnt Face travels and faces his challenges and from which he is rewarded. This is the world at the bottom of a lake to which a young man is led by the Elk. There he sees the suffering of the animals he had senselessly killed. This is the world in the sky to which a young girl is taken by her Star husband.

Inland Peoples, of course, live close to nature and have developed a rather pragmatic relationship with it. The thorn that pierces the fingertip is most assuredly felt and is to be avoided. But the thorn, the finger, and the pain are all given their very existence out of the structures and animations originating in the transcendent and told in the stories shared by the elders. The physical world is an overt manifestation of the spiritual inspirations and archetypes set forth and maintained by the myth people.

Several years ago I was introduced to the Crow term for clan, *ashammaléaxia.* The word literally means "as driftwood lodges." A Crow clan is a large assemblage of extended families related by matrilineal ties, from mother to daughter. As my association with Indian peoples has grown over the years, the term and the concept behind it have become more and more auspicious. For me, *ashammaléaxia* best introduces and encapsulates the Indian world view of the Inland Peoples.

As you look out into the rush of spring waters, the banks of the river just barely able to contain the turbulence, the Yellowstone offers a lesson. You see a piece of driftwood. It is submerged by an eddy, only to reemerge and be bashed against a protruding boulder. It does not fare well. But along the banks is another story. There you see driftwood in large numbers, each piece clinging to the other, each protected from the

Driftwood along the
Yellowstone River.

fast currents, the eddies, and the boulders. As the driftwood lodges, it thrives in a river of potential dangers.

The lesson is received. It is difficult to survive alone
in the river of life. Around the next bend an adversary
of some sort may await. But lodged together, as a
clan, each contributing to the others, the people hold
their adversaries at bay. Within the clan, all are given
importance—strong and weak, young and old, men
and women. All are needed if the lodging is to continue. Membership for each individual is maintained
through gift exchanges. As each gives to the others,
the driftwood lodges and reciprocates in kind. Those
participating in the exchanges—and thus lodged like
the driftwood—are "persons" of all kinds. The clan is
made up of not only human kinspeople, but of animal, bird, and plant peoples, and most importantly,
spirit peoples. Throughout one's life, an individual will

seek out and maintain ties with an *lilápxe,* a medicine father, a guardian spirit. As "respect" is given, a "child" is protected by a "father's" *baaxpée.* And the driftwood lodges together.[2]

I

COYOTE AND THE SWALLOWS
LOUIS SIMPSON, WISHRAM[3]

Coyote heard about two Sisters who had the fish preserved in their pond.
Then he went to them as they were collecting driftwood from the river.

He turned himself into a piece of driftwood.
He drifted along.
But they did not take hold of him.

He went ashore,
      ran off way yonder up river,
          and changed himself into a boy.
He put himself into a cradle,
      threw himself in the river,
          and again drifted along.

The two Sisters caught sight of him wailing.
They thought,
    "Some people have capsized,
        and this child is drifting towards us!"
The younger one thought,
    "Let us get hold of it."
But the older Sister did not want to have the child.
The child is drifting along.
The older Sister thought,
    "That is Coyote!"
Nevertheless the younger Sister took the child
    and put it in a canoe.

The two Sisters started towards their lodge.
The child was wailing,
    and they arrived home with it.
They took off the cradle

and looked at it closely.
As it turned out,
        the child was a boy.
The younger Sister said,
        "A boy is better than driftwood."

And then she went
        and cut an eel
                and put its tail in his mouth.
He straightway sucked at it
        and ate it all up.
She gave him another eel,
        and again he sucked at it,
                eating only half.
Then he fell asleep
        and half the eel was lying in his mouth.
The two women said,
        "He is asleep;
                now let us go for some more wood."

And then they went far way.
He arose and saw them going far off.
Then he made himself loose
        and seized their food.
He roasted the fish on a spit;
        when they were done,
                he ate.

He caught sight of the fish,
        which were their food,
                in a lake.
He examined the lake carefully,
        and discovered a spot where it could be easily broken.
"Here I shall make the fish break out,
        and then they will go to the Great River."[4]
He made five digging-sticks,
        from the wood of young oak.
And then he put them down in that place.

He started back home towards their lodge.

Again,
	just as before,
			he put himself into the cradle.
					Again there lay the eel's tail in his mouth.
Again he fell asleep.

Now the two Sisters arrived.
"The boy is sleeping,
	the boy is very good," they said.
And then they retired for the night.

Daylight came;
	the boy was sleeping.
Again the Sisters went for wood.
Again Coyote saw them going far way.
Then he got up
	and took their food.
He roasted it on a spit
	and ate it all up.

Then straightway he went to where his digging-sticks were.
Then he stuck his digger into the ground;
	he pulled it out,
			and the earth was all loosened up;
					his digging-stick broke.
He took hold of another one
	and again stuck it into the ground.
Then he loosened up the earth,
	and his digger was all broken to pieces.
He took hold of another one of his digging-sticks.
Again he stuck it into the ground;
	he loosened the earth all up,
			and his third digger was all broken to pieces.
He took hold of the fourth one;
	again his digger broke.
Now at last he took hold of the fifth
	and stuck it into the ground;
			he loosened the earth all up.
And then the fish slid over into the Great River.[5]

Now then the older Sister thought to herself.

Celilo Falls, September 1955. (Photo by Edwin Roby)

She said to her sister,
   "You said,
      'The child is good';
   I thought to myself,
      'That is Coyote.'
   Now this day Coyote has treated us badly.
   I told you,
      'Let us not take the child,
         that is Coyote.'
   Now we have become poor,
      Coyote has made us so."

Then the Sisters went to their lodge,
   and Coyote too went with them to their lodge.
He said to them,
   "Now by what right did you two keep these fish to yourselves?
   You two are birds,
      and I shall tell you something.
   Soon the people will come to this land.

Listen!"
And the people could be heard
    du'lululu.[6]
"Now they will come into this land;
    those fish will be the people's food.
Whenever a fish will be caught,
    you two will come.
Your name has become Swallows.
Now this day I have done this with you;
    thus I shall call you,
        'Swallows.'
When the people come,
    they will catch fish;
    and then you two Sisters will come,
    and it will be said of you,
        'The Swallows have come;
            Coyote called them.'
Thus will the people say,
    'Coyote took away the fish the two Sisters had captured in their pond;
    now the Swallows have come.'"

This is what Coyote called those two Sisters.

COYOTE AND THE SWEAT LODGE
Joe Hunt, Klikitat[7]

There was Coyote, his wife and his child.
Coyote would go about hunting;
    he would shoot and kill all sorts of things.

And now then he shot and killed a deer.
Then he butchered it.
There were two young ones in its belly.
He threw them away and left them there,
    at that place there.

The two young deer lay there.
And rain and snow came upon them.

And the Deer who he had killed felt very badly at heart about them.

Then after that Coyote went all over
    and shot and killed nothing.
He went all about tired.
He killed nothing.
And he went all about tired.

Then they became hungry.
And he thought,
    "Why is it that I do not shoot and kill anything?
    And now I shall defecate my two younger Sisters."
That is what he did.

And he said them,
    "Now you tell me!
        why I have I not killed anything?
    Now I am tired out.
    Now I am hungry."
And the younger Sisters said to him,
    "You always say,
        'That is the very thing I had forgotten about.'
    You go and figure it out!"
"Aha! Hurry up! Tell me!
    If you do not,
        then it will rain and the rain will break you up."
Then they answered,
    "Oh dear!
        We will tell you anyhow."
"Ready now! Hurry! Tell me!"
The Sisters told him,
    "Remember who you shot and killed,
        that deer,
    and whose fawns you left there at that place where they were
butchered,
        and which you left?
    The young fawns cried very much.
    Rain and snow came upon them
        and then it became cold.
    She who was their mother felt very bad at heart,

and then it became cold.
She who was their mother felt very bad at heart,
    the one you took home
She felt very, very badly at heart about you.
Then she must have gotten very angry.
That is why you never can kill.
But if you sweat for five days,
    after that you would become clean.
And then you may hunt.
And you will kill."
That is what the two Sisters said.
Coyote said in reply,
    "Oh, that is what I had been forgetting.
Ready now you!
Enter back into me, my younger Sisters."[8]
All right then.

Coyote went on and prepared a sweat house
    and sweated for five days,
        five bunches of rocks he used,
            one bunch for each of the five days.
After that Coyote went off.
    "Now I shall hunt the deer
        and I shall shoot and kill."

And then he went on and sure enough he found a deer,
    and shot and killed it.
And then he butchered it.
And he thought,
    "I shall not again leave young ones who are in the belly,
        for I shall take it all back home."
This Coyote did.
He took it all back home.

And after that he went about all the time,
    once again Coyote became a successful hunter.
Never did he hunger.

And that is what the two Sisters had told him,
    "If you bring back the game you have killed

and then you sweat immediately after you have returned
    home. . . ."
That is what Coyote did from then on.
    "All right then.
    That is how it will be for the people who are coming
        and will soon arrive here.
    And this is the way the people will do whenever they shoot
        and kill game.
    They will carry all of it back home.
    Nothing will they throw away.
    And always will they sweat for the purpose of the hunt.
    That is the way it shall be when the people have gotten here,
        they will soon be here.
    And then if they do not do this they will not shoot and kill game for
    many days.
    They will go about in vain,
        worn out.
    After that they should sweat.
    The sweat house will come first in importance for the people's hunting.
    With its help the people will be successful hunters.
    That is the manner it shall be."
Coyote decreed it would be.

|

COYOTE AND SWALLOWING
MONSTER
MARI WATTERS, NEZ PERCE[9]

Coyote . . . was going upstream.
Coyote is a-a-lways going upstream.
And . . he's going upstream,
    and he's going along the Clearwater
        and he noticed . . . that Salmon . . . were having some difficultly
        there,
            so, "*I'll* build a fish ladder so that the Salmon can go upriver
            and feed my people."[10]

And so he's busy working along there,
    and . . a Magpie flew over
        and says

"*Wha-a-t's you doin'*, Coyote?"
And Coyote looked up and says
    "*I-'m-m* building a fish ladder for the fish to go up, you know,
        to feed my people."
And . . . Magpie looked at him
    "*Ah-h-h-h*, there's *no reason* for the fish to go up there.
        The Monster, Its-welks, ate them all up.
           He's up in the valley,
                near Kamiah."
And Coyote says,
    "*Oh-h-h-h*, *that's* what happened to them.
    Oh, no wonder *nobody's* been around to help me."

So . . he starts up that way
    and he stops along the way
        and he takes a sweat bath.
He *cleans* himself up *re-e-al* nice, you know,
    and he says,
        "Well, I'd better sweat real good to get my *power*,
           and also to clean myself in case the Monster, . . .
              if he should *eat me* he won't find me repulsive!"
And so he takes a sweat bath.

And along the way he's going up over . . the Camas Prairie,
    and he stops
        and he gets some flint
           and makes some knives,
                flint knives,
        and makes something to start fire
           and he grabs some . . dry moss and things.
As he goes along,
    he gets some . . camas
        and some . . elderberries
           and other . . serviceberries
               and things like this
    and he puts them . . all in his . . . pack
And . . . he gets himself and he's on his way,
    and he's making these *ropes* out of hemp.
And he *goes* along,
    ah-h he's thinking of a plan.

He said,
        "Oh-h-h, I miss all my friends.
                I was wondering where Fox went, you know,
                        Oh-h-h"

So he . . gets up to the top of the prairie,
        "Well, . . . I'd better tie this rope around Mason Butte." . . .
And he goes and ties it around there
And he goes up and ties one rope around Seven Devil Mountains,
        and the other around . . . *Cottonwood* Butte . . .
And he ties them around his waist

And Coyote gets up to the Breaks and looking into Kamiah,
        and, "Ah-h-h, I don't want him to see me right away."
So he *covers* himself . . with clay
        and he's sort of . . . hard to see
And he *pe-e-e-ks* over the side there, you know,
        and spreads the weeds . . .
                and grass and what not
        and *lo-o-o-ks* over
                and sees the Monster.
Monster has just eaten a whole bunch,
        and he's sort of laying there . . . sleeping,
                with his head on his hands, you know,
                        sleeping away,
                                "Ah-ah-ah-ah." (whispering voice)

Coyote yells out, (whispering voice)
        "*Its-we-e-lks, Its-we-e-lks*!" . . (loud voice)
The Monster looks around,
        "*Who's* that? you know,
                who's that calling me?"
He looks around . . over . . the Breaks,
        and he can't see anybody.
Coyote is well-camouflaged . . .
And . . he says,
        "*Who is* that?"
And Coyote says,
        "*It's me*!" . . (louder)
Monster looks,

"'It's me'?
　　　Who's 'It's me'?
　　I don't know anybody named, 'It's me'!" . .
And Coyote *stood* up
　　and he said
　　　　"*It's me, Coyote.*" (loud voice)
"*Oh-h-h, there you are.*
　　What are you doing up there?" . .
"*Well,* I'm coming down
　　and we're . . going to test our powers out.
　　　　We're going to . . . see who's going to *draw* each other in." . . .
And the Monster,
　　"Haugh, haugh,
　　　　okay, alright, you go first.
　　We'll do it *three* times." . .

So Coyote gets up there
　　and he checks his ropes, you know,
　　　　and he's all tied up nice.
And he goes
　　"Ooh-ooh-ooh-ooh!"
And the only thing that happens is that maybe a hair on Monster's ear . . .
wiggles around.
"Haugh, haugh, haugh."

Coyote yells down at him
　　"*It's your turn,* Its-welks,
　　　　you try to suck me in."
So Its-welks opens his mouth and,
　　"Ooh-ooh-ooh-ooh!"
And the Coyote starts going down
　　but the ropes hold him back. . . .
And Its-welks looks
　　"*He-e-e-y*!
　　　　He's got a lot more power than I thought, you know!"

"Okay, it's your turn."
And Coyote gets up there,
　　"Ooh-ooh-ooh-ooh!"
A-a-a-nd nothing happens, you know

Monster goes
    "Hey-hey-hey-hey, haugh haugh haugh.
        I knew he couldn't do anything, you know.
        He thinks he's got power.
            I-'ve got more power."

And Coyote says
    "*Ok-a-ay, it's* your turn."
So . . Its-welks, he opens his mouth
    and drives in the *biggest* air.
        "Ooh-ooh-ooh-ooh-ooh-ooh."
And with that Coyote cuts some of the ropes
    and starts sli-i-ding down the hill, you know.
And the Monster's just about got him,
    maybe the next time . . .

"*Your* turn Coyote."
And Coyote,
    "Ooh-ooh-ooh-ooh."
And no-o-thing happened
    and Monster's sitting there,
        "*Hey-hey-hey*, haugh-haugh-haugh."

"*Ok-a-ay* get ready now!"
And he opens his mouth,
    "Ooh-ooh-ooh-ooh-ooh."
And Coyote goes *flying* through the air,[11]
    he reaches into his backpack,
        and throws out the roots and berries he brought with him.
And he says,
    "Soon, the human beings will be coming,
        and they will find these
        and be happy!"

And Coyote went *scootching* into his mouth, you know
"Aam-aam-aam-ay-ay-ay."
Its-welks lies down, . . .
    and he's content there

And Coyote is inside,

Heart of the Monster, near Kamiah, Idaho, ca. 1890. (Courtesy of the Idaho State Historical Society)

he gets his flint
  and makes a little torch
And he goes along,
  and . . sees all these animals,
    all these friends . . . and what not
and, "*Hello hello.*"
And they're glad to see him,
  some of them are jumping up and down.

And Old Grizzly Bear comes up,
  Bear comes up,
    "*Gra-ah, r-a-a-ah!*
      What are you doing here?
        I was going to save the people.
          You didn't have to come down."
And Coyote looks at him,
  "What are you getting so worked up for?
    You are so *ferocious* to *m-e-e,*
      why are you doing that?"
And pushed him in the nose, you know,
  pushed him back out of the way.
And that's why the Grizzly Bear has a different kind of nose than the Black
Bear! . .

And . . . he's going along with his light, you know,
  and Fox ran up to him.
"*Fox*, how are you?"
"I'm doing just fine!
  I was wondering when you were going to come and save us."
"Well, . . I need some help.

Coyote and Swallowing Monster / 57

You go and get all the boys together,
>and you have them gather all the bones of all the dead people,
>>and put them by all the openings,
>>>and then have them gather a-a-ll the wood
>>>>and bring it to the heart.
>But you have to show me where the heart is, you know."
And so Coyote goes on.

Fox runs on,
>and tells all the boys,
>>and they gather the bones of the dead people
>>>and they put them by *a-a-ll* the openings, you know.
They gather wood,
>and they show him where the *heart is* . .

But on the way there . . . they run into Rattlesnake,
>and Rattlesnake is just *mad* . . and *rattling*,
>>"Chish, chish, chish, . . . wish, chish, chish. . . . .
>>>*What* are you doing here?
>>>>I was going to save the people.
>>>>>I'm the one who has the *power*, you know"
And Coyote says,
>"*Oh*, you are so ferocious to everybody else,
>>and to me! you know.
>*Ah*, you are nothing but a *pest*!"
And *stepped* on his . . . head,
>and that's why a Rattlesnake has a flat head.
And he says,
>"From now on,
>>you're just going to be a *pest*.
>And you'll really be . . *scared* of people
>>and you'll *run away* when they come by.
>But . . . sometimes you'll be brave
>>and they'll *kill* you."
And that's what happens to rattlesnakes today! . .

But he found the heart.
Coyote takes pitch from his backpack,
>and starts a fire with the gathered wood under the Monster's heart.
He jumped on the heart.

Took one of his five knives out
    and he starts cutting away at the heart.
Smoke begins to come out the Monster's eyes,
    ears,
        nose
            and back end.

And as he cuts into the heart
    Its-welks, Monster,
        "O-o-oh, I'm getting heartburn.
        O-o-oh, I knew I shouldn't have eaten that Coyote,
        O-o-oh."
And he opens his mouth and some of his openings
    and . . . *a-a-ll* the boys throw out the bones,
        as many as possible.
And he keeps cutting,
    and every time he'd do that
        the Monster, Its-welks,
            "*O-o-o-oh*, o-o-oh."
And Coyote keeps cutting,
    and everything he does,
        that Monster,
            "*O-o-o-oh*,"
    and everything opens up
        and the boys throw out more bones.
Coyote breaks one knife,
    and then another,
        and finally he is down to his *last* knife, and what not.
Coyote keeps cutting away at the heart.
And he says to the people,
    "As soon . . as he opens up again,
        you all *run out*
            and I'll *run* out too, . .
               and he'll be *dead*."
So he cuts it and cuts it and cuts it,
    and finally the *last* knife breaks
        and the heart falls off.
And the Monster goes,
    "*O-o-o-o-o-oh*!"
And with that . . *everybody* runs out, . . .

out of his *nose,*
>   out of his *eyes,*
>   out of his *ears,*
>   out his *mouth,*
>   out of the *back end* . . .

And . . *Muskrat* . . was the last one to run out of the back end.
But he was *slo-o-ow* . .
And as the Monster died he closed his back end. . . . over the Muskrat's furry
tail,
>   *beautiful* furry tail.
And Muskrat,
>   "*Oh, no!*"
And he's sitting there, pulling his tail,
>   and he's pulled all his hair off.
And Coyote looked at him,
>   "*And* now what will you do?
>   We're *always* being the last one out.
>   You'll be just a scavenger the rest of your life!"
That's why Muskrat doesn't have any hair on his tail! . .

And at this point . . the . . . animals all are standing around
>   and . . . he starts . . . cutting the Monster up.
And gets some blood,
>   and . . . sprinkles it on the bones, . . .
>   and *a-a-ll* those . . dead people come to life.
And *everybody's* going,
>   "*Yeah, yeah,* yeah," you know.

Monster's all dead,
>   and . . . with the help of his friends,
>   they cut up the Monster,
>   and they throw different parts into different areas.
The feet landed over toward Montana
>   and that's where the *Blackfeet* came from.
Part of the head he threw over to another part of Montana,
>   and the *Flatheads*, you know, came over from there.
And . . . part of the tail,
>   they threw over to . . . the *Umatillas.*
And they threw some south,

the *Navajos*, . .
　　and the *Shoshone*,
　　　　and every place . . else.
They threw part of the belly over into Montana
　　and that's the *Assiniboine* . . the "*big bellies*!"
And . . . ah, he was busy just *throwing* meat every which way,
　　parts of the Monster

And Fox comes up to him and says, . . .
　　"*What about* the *people here?* . . .
　　　　You forgot all about them."
The only thing left was the heart,
　　the kidney,
　　　　and a breast.
I guess the Monster was a woman.
Anyway,
　　and he says,
　　　　"*Oh*, I forgot *a-a-ll* about that. . . .
　　　　　　Go get some water from this clear . . . river,
　　　　　　　　the Clearwater."
And he got him water.
"Now *pour* it over my hands."
And Coyote washed his blood off, you know,
　　and it dripped down.
He said,
　　"Where this blood . . . lands
　　　　and with this heart will grow a people . . .
　　　　　　They'll be *strong*.
　　　　　　　　They'll be *brave*.
　　　　　　　　　　They'll have *good* hearts.
　　　　　　　　　　　　They will lead good lives.
　　And these will be the Nez Perce." . .
And that's where the Nez Perce came from . . .

|

SEAL BOY
ANONYMOUS, WASCO[12]

The people,
　　who lived at the mouth of the Columbia River,

moved some distance to the east.
At the end of the first day's journey they camped on the shore.
One of the men had a little boy.

After they had fixed the camp,
    he went with the boy to mend his canoe.
After awhile the boy disappeared.
    The father thought he had gone back to the camp.

When he had finished the canoe,
    he went to the camp
        and asked his wife where the boy was.
She had not seen him.

They went to the river,
    tracked him to the water,
        and all said that he was drowned.
Next morning the people moved on still farther up the river.
The parents hunted everywhere for the child,
    but at last they too went;
        they could not find the child.

Two or three years after this another party went up the river.
On an island in the river there were a great many seals,
    and among them a boy.
Word was sent to the parents of the boy.
People went out and watched for the seals to come to land,
    so that they might see the boy.
They watched till the seals came up on the island,
    one by one,
        and soon the island was covered.

At last the boy came up out of the water
    and lay down by the seals.
The people crept up,
    caught the boy,
        and took him to shore by force.
He struggled to get away from them,
    and tried to return to the water.

At first he refused to eat anything but raw salmon and other fish,

and he would not talk.
But by degrees he came to act like other human beings.
Finally his parents got him back to his right mind,
    and he became very industrious.
He carved bows and arrows
    and worked all the time.

As he grew up,
    he used to tell many stories of how he had lived down with the seals.
He said that seals were just like people.
They moved from place to place,
    camped at night,
        and would go as far as The Dalles.
They moved around as the Indians did on land.

The people had to watch him when he was in a canoe,
    for fear he would go back to the seals.
The seals were always floating around when he was near.
He always called them by name.
His parents always covered his head when he was in a canoe.

One day he threw the cover off,
    saw the seals,
        called them by name,
    said,
        "I am going,"
    and jumped into the water.
He came to the surface far out,
    and said to his father and mother,
        who were in the canoe,
    "I have a home down in the water.
        I will remain there from now on."

Literary Motifs

As with cultural themes, there are a variety of literary motifs that can be readily identified in the oral literature. Two of the prominent are the trickster and the orphan quest.[13]

The Trickster

It is in the figure of Coyote, or *Smi-yiw,* as the Coeur d'Alene call him, that we see the trickster character par excellence. He is the transformer who uses his powers, intellect, and cunning to affect the world around him. In the instance of the Crow, it is *Isáahkawuattee,* Old Man Coyote, who calls on his younger brother, Hell Diver, to bring up a little mud from the bottom of the waters that cover the entire world. With this earth, Old Man Coyote travels across the country, bringing forth the mountains and rivers and creating the animals and plants. Finally, with the advice of younger brother Little Fox, he molds from the earth and blows life into the human peoples. They are created so that someone can "appreciate Coyote's creation!"

Among the peoples of the Plateau, it is Coyote who travels up the Columbia and its various tributaries, "always going upstream," transforming the land. Animal and plant peoples are given their particular characteristics and behaviors. Hunting methods, social customs, and sacred ceremonies are defined. He is a culture hero. Among the Pend d'Oreille, it is Coyote who slays the dangerous Snake Monster. Today the Monster's body parts can be seen throughout the Flathead valley in Montana. The mouth is near Ravalli, the heart at a butte near Jocko, the tail near Evero and the poles Coyote brought with him while inside the Monster are the two tamaracks seen growing near Arlee. A world raw and dangerous is redefined in preparation for the "coming of the people." And as wonderfully illustrated in the Nez Perce story of Coyote and the Swallowing Monster, it is Coyote who creates the various human peoples from the body and blood of the Monster.

But there are other sides to Coyote. As witnessed in the Kootenai creation story, "The Animals and the Sea Monster," for instance, Coyote's omnipotence is not always evident. While acknowledged as the "fastest runner," Coyote is not the one who kills the Sea Monster and creates the human peoples; rather, he himself is almost swallowed! While he is a primary transformer of the world, his actions are not always benevolently motivated. Much of his inspiration is predicated on his insatiable hunger and amorous desires. It is Old Man Coyote's greed that sends him running away with "younger brother's little bell" as well as with the "fine dart" he had just traded to the younger brother for the bell. And it is Coyote's desire for "the most beautiful woman" that results in his own demise.

In order to realize these less noble desires, Coyote engages in games of inventiveness, strategy, and deception, attempting to outwit an opponent in order to maximize his gains and to minimize his losses. He is an active agent, asserting himself over his environment and his opponents, applying his great skills of trickery and deception. The world Coyote travels is full of adversaries and dangers. It can be a very hostile world.

It should be noted that this is also the Coyote whose actions are venerated in certain situations and who sets a behavioral example for humans. This is clearly the case in the "accomplishments" of Wise Man. In the Crow story, Wise Man, a warrior, is "out looking for the enemy," attempting to "count coups on them," a trickster in a dangerous land. Wise Man's particular deception is guided by the character of Coyote.

Yet Coyote's schemes to have a "great feast" or to possess the "good-looking girl" usually end in his being duped by his own trickery or outwitted by his opponent. He is made the fool. Coyote may even find himself "dead," to be revived only when his companion, Fox or Mrs. Mole, for instance, comes along and jumps over him three times. (Once revived, Coyote invariably admits only to having been "asleep!")

When Coyote's intentions are to assist others, "prepare for the coming of people," he generally succeeds; when his intentions are for himself alone, he is likely to fail. But even in the failure, Coyote offers important lessons to those listening to his story. He sets forth what one *should* or *should not* do in certain situations: "You have to listen to what people tell you;" "Things aren't always greener on the other side!"; "If you . . . give something to a white man, and it's going to do him some good . . . , he'll skin you alive! . ." And in his failures, Coyote plays the comic fool, bringing much-needed laughter.

While Coyote usually relies on himself, he is sometimes assisted by his "helpers." When a course of action is unclear or something is left incomplete, Coyote may consult with Fox, as he does among the Coeur d'Alene, Crow, and Sanpoil. Among certain Plateau peoples—the Klikitat, Nez Perce, and Sanpoil, for example—Coyote is assisted by some "unusual helpers." When Coyote is unable to reach a decision, he may bring forth his excrement Children or Sisters. Initially, these "offspring" may refuse to help, but when Coyote threatens them with rain that would wash them away, they generally offer advice, only to be told by Coyote, "I knew that all along!"[14]

The Orphan Quest

In contrast to the assertive, deceptive, and often self-serving Coyote is the character expressed in the orphan quest. This motif combines universal literary elements of the "culture hero" and the "animal parent." Within the narrative, the motif often unfolds with an individual falling into orphan status, becoming impoverished and destitute, separated from parents and family, as in "Seal Boy." Perhaps the individual is abused, a victim of repeated attacks by the village "bully." In "Burnt Face," the "orphan" has been badly scarred. Among the Crow, such an imperfection can keep an individual from reaching full social status. Thus the status of orphan can be either symbolic or literal.

Falling into impoverishment, the individual may take part in a "quest" or become accidently lost and abandoned by his people. In either instance, the orphan becomes totally removed from the world of human peoples, and enters a "liminal period," "betwixt and between." Alone in the mountains, "far from the dwelling places of humans," the quester gives of himself in sacrifice. Ironically, it is one who has little to give who must give even more. Challenges await. He may have

Cedars near the Coeur
d'Alene River, Idaho.

to go without food and water for a certain number of days. A dangerous "monster" may have to be slain. For Burnt Face, his adversary is the Long Otter. Above all, the quester must be "sincere" and respectful, must give of his "heart."

If the gift from the quester is judged worthy, an animal parent will visit and "adopt" him. Reciprocity occurs. The world now entered is full not of potential adversaries but of omnipotent allies. The animal, as a spirit guardian, may appear in a vision to offer instructions and power. The lost child may be taken in by the Little People or the Buffalo People and raised as one of their own. A disfigurement may be removed. The power to overcome a "bully" may be given. The animal people provide what has been denied by the human people. An individual is no longer orphaned, but "adopted" into an extended family of "persons."

In affirmation of the newly acquired status, the individual returns to his camp triumphant. His new status is acknowledged. The "bully" is subdued. The disfigured individual is accepted by others. And, as expressed among the Crow, the individual lives "to such an old age that when he moves his skin would tear—that's old!"

We will see the orphan quest motif clearly expressed in both accounts of "Burnt Face," as well as in "The

Couple Befriended by the Moon." In the stories of "Little Head," "Seal Boy" and "Elk and the Young Man," elements of the orphan quest motif will also be glimpsed.

It is of interest to note that the literary elements of the orphan quest motif replicate the behavioral process found in any "rite of passage." The orphan quest is readily exemplified in the actions of those who participate in a Coeur d'Alene vision quest or the Crow Sun Dance ceremony, for example. The model of action and resolution first set forth by the myth people continues to find expression in the lives of human peoples. There is thus a strong correspondence between myth and ritual.

There are four structural components within any rite of passage: orphaned status, separation and quest, vision and adoption, and affirmation and rebirth.

1. **Orphaned status.** An incompleteness is identified—sickness in oneself or in a loved one or youthful immaturity, for example. The individual is called *eechełm* by the Coeur d'Alene, roughly "I've been left alone by my parents" or "by the medicine powers."

2. **Separation and quest.** Boys of fifteen or sixteen years of age are encouraged to "discover" the "great mysteries," to seek a vision that will guide them throughout their lives. In prayer, a vow is made to give of the self. Two, three, or four days of sacrifice might be offered. The individual is removed from the ordinary and mundane. A purification through a sweat bath, rubbing the body with "sweet man-sage," or incensing with sweet cedar might initiate the quest. The site for the quest is typically a far-off butte or mountain ridge. There, a wall of rock and bed of sweet sage is prepared, "to keep strangers away." With the tobacco of a cigarette or kinnikinnick in a traditional pipe, prayer is given. "As the smoke ascends, so too do the words!" The quester hum-

bles himself, showing humility and going without food and water. The quester is "drying up," offering up that which sustains his life. Most importantly, he does this with "heart" and "sincerity," what the Crow call *díakaashe,* "he/she is really doing it" with "determination and pride." A sacrifice is made; a gift is given.

3. **Vision and adoption.** If the quester's gift is judged worthy and accepted, a healing or a vision is rendered. An animal person takes "pity" on the quester. A loved one is healed perhaps. A "dream vision" transpires, what the Coeur d'Alene term *qis.* Where there had been two active agents—the quester offering up a sacrifice and a guardian spirit judging its worth—during a vision there is a union, the two become one. The individual journeys with or as part of the guardian spirit, the *ansh* to the Couer d'Alene—an Eagle, a Buffalo, an Elk, or one of the Little People. Ordinary time and space are dissolved during a vision experience. The visionary communicates with a spirit guardian, learning of spiritual truths and being given personal guidance, and possibly acquiring spiritual power, *súumesh.* The quester is adopted, gaining in spiritual kinship. In order to maintain this paternal relationship, rules of respect and taboos associated with the guardian spirit are specified. One should not eat of the meat of a certain animal or a sweat bath should be taken at particular times in one's life, for instance. Gifts must continue to be given.

4. **Affirmation and rebirth.** After the vision experience, the individual journeys back to the world of human peoples, having regained new status in their eyes, now an adult in "good health." To continue the kinship with the adopted spirit guardian, prayers and songs are given each day. They are often directed through the objects assembled in a medicine bundle—feathers, a braid of

sweet grass, a rock, or other representations of the newly established spirit relationship. Respect must continue.

Salmon River near Challis, Idaho.

We have a unique opportunity to view the orphan quest motif expressed in two versions of the Crow story "Burnt Face." One account is from Plenty Hawk, recorded by Robert Lowie in 1916. The second account was told to me in 1993 by Tom Yellowtail. In presenting both versions of the story of Burnt Face, I am not implying that one account is somehow more "correct" than the other. Though the accounts are separated by over seventy years of time, they are both considered "true." As Tom mentioned to me at the conclusion of his telling of "Burnt Face," "and this is a true story." They refer to differing persons and situations, but they are reflective of the same literary motif. Indeed, embedded in both are similar quintessential metaphoric and anagogic significances that speak to the importance of the quest, the value of self-sacrifice and reciprocity and of respect for the "higher powers" upon whom we depend.

I am reminded of a storytelling at a Crow Sun Dance encampment some fifteen years ago. We had just been treated to a wonderful telling of a buffalo-day story involving an orphaned boy adopted by a group of Little People who lived near Pryor Gap. When the story was finished, another accomplished storyteller objected, "Oh, no! It wasn't the Little People but the Buffalo People who took the boy in." This is not to lessen the idiosyncratic influences differing family traditions will have on the same story, which will inevitably take on the influence of the one who tells it and reflect the period and place where it is told. While we may cling to the notion of a singular, literal truth, history lends its own uniqueness. Whether told by Plenty Hawk or Tom Yellowtail, at the mythic level a story such as "Burnt Face" reveals the same archetypal orphan quest motif, and reflects the the same truth.

|

COYOTE AND THE ROCK
Lawrence Aripa, Coeur d'Alene[15]

And so . . one day . . the Coyote . . was . . enjoying the day
    enjoying himself.
He is out . . by the . . . Spokane valley now, . .
    and he was going along the river . . *just* happy as can be,
        "Hey yaa yaa aa, hey hey yaa yoo, yaa aa!"
            Happy! happy! happy! (rapid phrasing followed by smiles
            and light laughter from audience)
    And nothing, nothing could spoil his fun.

And all of a sudden . . here came . . . a *bird*, . .
    all beat up . . .
"Help, I need help!" (in a very weak voice)
And he looked over in the other . . direction
    and here come another one, . .
"I need help!" (again in a weak voice)

all beat up,
        a-a-ll scratched,

And then . . all of a sudden there was many . . beings . . came to him,
    and they says,
        "Coyote, we need your help! . .
"What's the matter?"
"There is a *big Rock* . . that is . . really . . doing . . harm to everything
    everybody. (slow deliberate voice, rolling the words out)
    He is angry,
        and he . . is just, just,
            he is ruining everything.
    He is knocking down lodges,
        he is knocking down trees.
    He is just doing *bad* things.
        You have to stop him,
            because we know you . . have special powers . . from the
            animal spirits."
So the Coyote,
    "Well, . . what's in it *for me?*" . . (laughter from audience)
And so . . they says,
    "Well, . . Coyote, . . if you do this for us . . we will give you anything
    you want,
        you want mice?
            you want snakes?
                we'll give it to you.
    Anything that you want,
        but get rid of that *Rock*
            as he is doing a lot of damage." . . .
So the Coyote says,
    "Alright, *I'll do it!*"

So he goes . . looking around,
    and all of a sudden . . he sees *all* the wreckage . . around him.
And he says
    "A-a-h, now I'm on the *trail!*"
So he goes.

And then . . here is the Rock . . .
He is *mad*

he is just, just *mean.*
And he is *rolling*
    and *hitting* everything,
        knocking everything over,
    and he don't care *what* he rolls over
        or, or *what* he does . . .

And then the Coyote says,
    "Well, . . . how can I get him?" . .
He says,
    "A-a-h, if I get him *r-e-ally angry*
        and have him *chase* me.
    And I can go somewhere . . where I can finally get rid of him."

And so . . he goes up to the Rock,
    and he starts making fun of him
        and doing *all kinds of things* . . .
And the Rock gets mad,
    and he says,
        "*Coy-o-te, I am going to get chou!*" (in a deep, low angry voice
        rising in volume)
So he goes after the Coyote.

The Coyote is very fast.
So he jumps over here,
    jumps over there, (rapid voice as if hopping)
        and *he's laughing.*
"Come and get me,
    come and get me."
And . . the more he hollers, . .
    the more the Rock gets angry.

All of a sudden the Rock is jumping here
    and there,
And all of a sudden . . he's created mountains . .
    all the way back,
        Mount Spokane
            and all of these others
                because of the way he jumps.
The earth would come up

or the earth would go down
                    or he would just *roll about* slowly,
                              and that is where the flat parts came.
But he couldn't catch the Coyote.

And the Coyote says,
          "This is all good
                    but . . how can I get *rid* of him though? (slow questioning voice)
                              How can I get rid of him for *good*?
          He's still . . .
                    he's raising . . heck,
                              he's doing everything *bad*!" . .
So . . he says,
          "Well, over . . way over here . . there's a lake,
                    maybe I can go over there.
          And then . . I can get rid of him in the water." . .
So he hides.
And then the Rock can't find him.

The Rock looks around.
He, he *tries* to find the Coyote.
And then all of a sudden the Coyote hollers,
          "*Here I am*, . .
                    here I am!" (in a weak as if distant voice)
And then . . the Rock sees him
          and he goes over,
And then . . the *race* begins . . .

The Rock is after the Coyote.
And the Coyote goes over the mountains.
And as the Rock is rolling,
          he is picking up all kinds of things.
                    He is running over . . *huckleberries,*
                              he ran over a great . . big . . patch of huckleberries.
          And the Rock turned blue,
And he is just a goin',
          just . . trying to catch that Coyote.
But couldn't do it,

And the Coyote . . thought,

"Now, what can I do?
I've got to get rid of him."
And he was getting tired.
So he says,
"Oh, I remember.
There is a large cliff over here.
If I can jump on the edge of that cliff
and let the Rock go over,
I'll be safe!"

So he *did that*.
He run like. . . . *crazy*, (long pause followed by laughter from audience)
he run as fast as he could. (laughter continues)
He got to the edge of the cliff
and he jumped down in a little,
a little place there to hide.

And here's the Rock, . .
all blue
just a rollen'
just *mad*.
And he goes
he goes over the cliff,
down he goes
And he *rolls* and *rolls*
He goes into the lake. . . .

And . . that's . . why . . Coeur d'Alene Lake . . is *blue*! (very slow and
deliberate voice followed by tremendous audience laughter)

|

COYOTE AND THE DART
YELLOW-BROW, CROW[16]

It's Old Man Coyote.
He is going around,
very hungry.
He gets to Little Fox,
running across slippery ice.
He has a little bell tied to the end of his tail.

As he runs on the ice,
    it strikes the ice.
Little pockets of warm tallow are there.
Little Fox retraces his steps and picks the tallow out.
He eats it.

Old Man Coyote watches him,
    "My dear younger brother, Little Fox,
        what you own is wonderful!
    Do it for me."
"Why, I need this bell.
    I get my food from it.
    I won't give it up," Little Fox says.
"Give me your bell, younger brother!"
"It is most valuable to me."
"I'll give you my fine dart!
    If I give you my dart,
        give me your bell."
Little Fox likes the dart.
"Well, alright,
    I'll trade with you, older brother."

Old Man Coyote ties the bell to his blanket,
    goes out over the ice.
He runs on the ice,
    the bell strikes the ice and holes are filled with fat.
He turns around,
    takes it,
        eats it.
He likes it!

Little Fox is holding his dart.
It is Old Man Coyote who comes along.
"My younger brother,
    I'd like to look again at my dart I owned.
    It's no longer part of me,
        but please give me my dart,
            I want to look at it again,
        then I'll go my way."

Then he gives it to him.

Old Man Coyote takes it and examines the dart.
Then he says,
    "Ha, Ha!"[17]
            runs away.
    "Long ago I used to do this for fun."
He runs away.

The Little Fox says,
    "Old Man Coyote, don't do it four times!"
Old Man Coyote says,
    "Just now I've told you that I used to do this long ago."[18]
"Nevertheless I have said it."
Little Fox walks away.

Old Man Coyote goes on and reaches his lodge.
The ice is slippery.
    He goes there.
"Well, Ancient Man,[19]
    you are very hungry,
        for some time you have not done anything.
If your hunger is satisfied,
    it will be."
He reaches the ice.

He goes round a bend of the river,
        there is a second bend,
            still he goes around.
He stops.
"Do this,
    keep on eating what is there,
        that's the way."
He turns back,
    picks up the tallow as he goes.
He retraces his steps,
    he eats up all the fat.
"That's the way,
    keep on roaming about,

Ancient Man."
Old Man Coyote roams about.

After a while he has done it three times.
Toward the end of his third trail he slips forward
    and almost falls,
        but then he regains his balance and stands up.
"Well!
    My bottom moved,
        now we'll stop."
He stops,
    turns around,
        picks up the fat,
            eats it all.
"Come on,
    your hunger is satisfied."
He keeps on roaming about.

Then he gets very hungry.
"Come, Ancient Man,
    we have become very hungry again,
        we'll get to the river and feast."
He goes and gets to the river.
The ice is very slippery.
He ties this bell to the lower part of his blanket.
He goes running on the ice.
As he goes,
    he slips,
        his bottom strikes the ice and sticks to it.
He remains there unable to help himself.
He sits on the ice,
    in vain he tries to get free.

A Prairie-chicken comes there.
"My dear younger brother,
    come, I have an idea now."
"Well, what is it, elder brother?"
"Let us have a pleasant dance.
    You have big pouches,
        the space inside is pretty big,

go ahead and fill them with rose berries,
    keep on pouring them out," Coyote says.
He keeps pouring out plenty of rose berries,
    there is plenty.

A Beaver comes there.
"My dear younger brother,
    come here,
        I want to invite that one,
            bring me an instrument to sing with!"
"Yes, what shall I do?"
"Bunch willows.
    Your teeth are sharp,
        gnaw an armful and bring it!"
"How long shall I make it?"
"This size make it."
He judged it,
    he made the right size.
"Here it is," he says,
    and gives it to him,
        laying it down.

"Hello, Magpie,
    come, my younger brother."
He comes and gets there.
"What is it, my elder brother?"
"Speak for me, please,
    you have a loud voice:
        'That Old Man Coyote wants to feast you,
            he calls you,
                he invites you.
      Beavers,
         Skunks,
            Cottontails,
                Jackrabbits,
                    Prairie dogs,
                      Porcupine,
    it is you animals whose feet touch the ground that he invites.'
    You, Prairie chickens,
        rose berries are your food

and it's not yet the season for you to dance,
but if you dance,
you are the ones I most want to see.
When you are through dancing,
you'll eat plenty," Old Man Coyote says.

He took this stick.
"Hey there,
I'll tell you something," Old Man Coyote says.
"Yes," they say.
"When I sing,
then all of you shut your eyes!
At the height of my song,
go under my bottom."
"Yes," they say.

Then when he is at the height of his song,
they go under his bottom that's stuck to the ice.
It's loose.
Old Man Coyote casts about for the fattest animals,
hits them severely on the top of their ears,
knocking them down.

He tries to get a very fat one-eyed Prairie dog to come closer.
It never does.
"One-eyed Prairie dog,
what's the matter?
It's you I want to show off,
come close to me and dance,
I want to see you above all,
come at least once!" Old Man Coyote says.
This Prairie dog comes over,
first half-shutting his eyes,
he watches him.
He comes,
he jumps back,
he glances.
As soon as he opens his eyes,
he sees his friends strewn about.
"What! Old Man Coyote has been destroying us!

Absaroka Mountains near the Yellowstone River, in southern Montana.

Save yourselves!" he cries,
> he goes inside a crack in the ice.
The rest separate and flee.
Whatever he did thus he gets a good meal.
He gets up,
> builds a fire and cooks.
He has a good meal.

COYOTE AND THE WHITE MAN
LAWRENCE ARIPA, COEUR D'ALENE[20]

Coyote was going along, . . .
> and all of a sudden . . . he heared a *man screaming*,
> > "He-lp, help, help!"
> and he says
> > "That's a strange *voice*?"
> He says,
> > "That isn't an Indian!
So he runs over and he looks,
> and there . . . is a White Man,
> > the *first* one he's ever seen.
> And the White Man . . is getting beat up . . by a group of Indians. . . .
And so they are just about ready to kill him
> they are *really* going after him.

And the Coyote says
    "*Well*, I still have a *little power*,
            maybe I can chase them away?"

So Coyote goes to his tipi,
        and makes some "Indian ice cream,"
                from berries and what not.
It's all foamy
        and he puts it all over his mouth. (motions with hands over his mouth).
            like he has *rabies*!21

So he jumps up there,
        and he *scares* them,
        and he says,
            "I will use my powers
                    and I will get rid of *all of you*,
                        you leave the man alone!"
So they did,
        they left him alone . . .

And the man was grateful,
        "Thank you,
            I don't know who you are
                but I am *grateful*,
                    thank you for what you've *done* for me."
And he says
        "That's alright."
He says
        "I'm the *Coyote*.
                And I am lonely."
He says
        "I can't . . use my powers anymore,
            and people,
                they ignore me now
                    they don't depend on me
                        and nobody will pla-a-y with me
                            nobody will listen to my stories!"
And he says,
        "I am *getting lonely*!" . . .
And the man says,

"Well, . . I can keep you company."
He says,
        "I can do anything that will make you happy,
                because you saved *my* life."
So the Coyote says,
        "Well, stay with me!". .
And he did.

A-a-ll summer long . . they enjoyed each other's company,
        they *had a lot* of fun,
                they went swimming,
                        they went
                                and did all different kinds of things.
        And they had a-a-ll the *food* they wanted.
And so the two of them got along real well.

And then all of a sudden . . the summer was gone.
        The leaves turned,
                and everything got *co-o-ld*.
And then it was winter time.
They didn't go out
        and get food
                and save it.
So here they were
        no food, . . .
                and they were starving. . . .
And so they said,
        "*Well, what can we do?*
        We have to do something to get *food* otherwise we will both perish.". .
So the Coyote says
        "Well, . . . about fifty miles up this way,
                a . . they tell me that they're starting a *trading post* over there."
He says
        "Maybe we can go
                and *trade*
                        and get some food from the man *there*?"
So the man says
        "Alright, so let's *go*!"

So they went and they started off,

Beaver country, St. Joe River, northern Idaho.

and they were *v-e-ry hungry,*
      almost starving.
They got close,
    and the Coyote says
        "Now, I have a plan."
He says,
    "You tie my four legs together
        and put me over your shoulder
            and go up to the *trading post*
            and tell the man that you want to trade . . coyote hide . . for some
        food!"
And he says
    "And when, you *get* the food,
        you come back out and untie me.
    And then we will just leave,
        and we will have a-a-ll that food
        and it will keep us, . . .
            for most of the winter."
So the man says
    "*Al*right, okay!"

So they get close
    and then he ties up his legs
        and puts him on his shoulder
            and then he goes up
    and all of a sudden the trader comes out,

"O-o-o-oh, look at that,
    that's a *be-e-autiful fur*,
        where did you get it?"
The man says,
    "I got it
        I trapped it,"
and says,
    "I want to *trade*, . . .
        if it's *possible?*"
And the man says,
    "*Su-u-re!*"
He looked at it,
    "I can give you about twenty dollars worth of food."
And the man says
    "Oh, good!"
So he lays the Coyote down
    and they go into the trading post.

The Coyote is laying there
    and listening . . .
All of a sudden he hears the man say, . . .
    "I want that . . *sugar*,
        I want *coffee*,
            I want bre-e-ad,
                all of the good things,
                    G-e-e-z-z!"
Coyote is laying there,
    and he is *gett-en' hungry.* (laughter from audience)
"*A-a-h*," he says,
    "He's getten' all the things that I like."
And he says,
    "Boy, now when he comes out,
        we can go and we will *eat*,
            and we will both get our strength back,
                and *everything will be fine.*" . .

And then he heard the man make the deal,
    and so . . . the man comes out,
        and he and the trader . . . shake hands,
            and then he comes by the coyote.

Coyote and the White Man / 85

Here he has . . a big . . . bundle of . . . *f-o-o-d.*
He has *a-a-ll the things* that the Coyote likes to eat.

And he comes by,
    and then the Coyote *looks* at him,
        "S-s-s-s-p, untie me!" (whispering voice)
And the man don't even look at him,
    keeps walking.
"S-s-s-p, *hah, hah,*
    you're suppose to untie me!" (much louder and almost desperate voice)
The man keeps walking
    don't even *hear him,*
        he just keeps right on a walkin'.

All of a sudden he's getting out there by himself
    and the Coyote starts hollering
        "Hay, you come back here,
            you come back here,
                or I'll catch up to you, . . .
                    and chew out . . your windpipe,
        you come back here!" (desperate voice)
And . . the man didn't even hear him.

All of a sudden the door opens
    and the trader come out,
        and he looks,
            "I thought I heard *voices!"* . . .
So he looked around,
    and he don't se-e-e anything.
And then he thought,
    "Oh it's *that man,*
        he's so happy to get *food* that he's singing,
            he's *way up* there by himself
                and he's *enjoying it."*
He says,
    "Ah, I'm glad . . I was able to make that man . . happy."

He looks down,
    and there's the Coyote.
The Coyote is, is *mad,*

and he's *scared,*
>   and he's laying there with his eyes shut.
And the man goes back into . . the trading post,
>   and in a couple of minutes he comes out,
>> and he's got a sharpener,
>>> and he's got a *la-a-rge knife*
>> and he's going
>>> su-u-wsh, su-u-wsh, su-u-wsh, su-u-wsh. (audience laughter)
He's sharpening it up.
And the Coyote looked up,
>   "*U-u-u-u-h,* . . . *I'm going to get it.*" (a lot of audience laughter)
And he says,
>   "*You can't do that!*"
The man stops,
>   he looks around,
>> "I thought I heard a voice?" (a few laughs)
And the Coyote says,
>   "*Don't kill me,*
>> *don't, don't skin me*!" (pleading voice)
And the man goes down,
>   takes his knife,
>> he can't he-a-r.
So he . . goes right ahead,
>   and he skins the Coyote . . .

And the Coyote has *no* skin.
He looks *pi-ti-ful,* . .
>   he's already *skinny*! (audience laughter)
The man takes him,
>   throws him . . . in the pile of . . . brush and everything.

And there's the po-or Coyote.
He can't *m-o-ve*
>   and he can't *hol-ler*
>> and he's *gone*! . .
And so . . that is the end . . of the Coyote.
And he laid there
>   and *he* was *just dead.*

And all of a sudden Mr. Fox comes by.

And Mr. Fox comes,
 goes over,
  and Mr. Fox is *wi-se*! . .
   "Oh, that po-or thing." . .
He says,
 "Well, he's no good sometimes.
  He's mischievous.
   He has no respect for others.
 But, *a-a-h*, sometimes he's *pretty good*!"
He says,
 "Well, maybe I'll bring him back to life."

So he takes him,
 and he lays him on the ground,
  and then he prays, . . .
   "Animal spirit, . . give me *your powers,*
    help me so I can bring this foolish thing back to life
    . . . (chuckle by storyteller and laughter by audience)
   Maybe he don't deserve it
    but he *is* . . . my friend.
   And so *help* me."
So he dances around . . the body
 and he goes around and sings
  and then he gets over
   and he *jumps* over . . once . .

And then when he *jumps over* he stops,
 "*What* am I do-o-ing?
  That Coyote is only goin' to raise . . . a lot of *trouble* if I bring
 him back!"
And then he turns and he looks
 "*Well*, . .
  I guess I *can* . . . help him."
So he jumps over again.

But he is still puzzled,
 "I *shouldn't do this,*
  he's just a mischievous
   a no-good . . . Coyote!"
And then he says,

"No, I have to do it."
So he jumps over the third time.

And the Coyote opens his eyes, . .
    he stretches,
        and *"A-a-a-a-h, I've slept a-a-long time!"*
And the Fox looks at him,
    "Sleep? . . .
        You've been dead!
    You *foolish* thing
        don't you know that, that you did . . something *wr-o-ong?*
    And now you are . . are *go-o-ne*
        but I have brought you back!"
And the Coyote sat there,
    and he says,
        "O-o-o-h, now I remember.
He says
    "A-a-a-h that man, . . .
        that man, he's the one . . . that had me killed,
            and he wouldn't help me when . . he should of
                and he took *a-a-ll* the *food."*
And he says,
    "I'm going to catch up to him
        and I'm going to *chew* his windpipe."
Mr. Fox says,
    "Wait, *wait,* Coyote, . . .
        you were *dead.*
    You have to be *thankful* that you are *a-live now,*
        that you are able to *breathe*
            you're going to be able to *eat*
                you'll be able to . . . do *all the things* that you did
                before.
    And you should be *grateful.*
    And I am telling you . . . as a friend,
        don't, don't do anything, . . .
            don't look for *revenge.*
    Just live . . the way you have to live!"
And so he preached on and on.

And then . . . the Coyote says,

Yucca near Pryor, Montana.

"Yes, . . . *you're* right."
He says,
"Okay, I *won't* chew out . . his windpipe,
I won't do anything.
Alright, I'll change.
I'll be a *go-o-d, go-o-d Coyote* from now on."
And Mr. Fox says,
"I'm glad you feel that way."
He says
"But let this be a lesson to you." . .
He says
"Now remember, . . .
from this time on . . . there are going to be *a-a lot* of white men
that come."

And he says
    "And I want you to *remember*, . . .
        now *remember* this, ...
            if you . . . give something to a white man,
                and it's going to do him some good, . . .
        he'll skin you alive! . . . (slow deliberate voice, followed by tre-
        mendous laughter from audience)

And so that . . was another lesson that we had to learn. . . .
And we haven't *yet*! . . . (more laughter from both storyteller and audience)

|

WISE MAN
Tom Yellowtail, Crow[22]

A few men,
    possibly four or five men, . .
        in this little war party, . .
            that were traveling . . (in a very slow pace and deliberate
            voice, long pauses between morphemes)
Among them . . . was *Wise Man*,
    the Indians called him, . .
        very wise, . . .
            very smart . . . as we might say, . .
            among his Indian people.
And we respect him . . for the wise things . . . he's done . . .

So . . in this war party . . a few men,
    possibly five . . six men,
        just a few, . .
            that were . . out . . traveling,
                looking for the enemy . . .
And over hills . . they were traveling, . .
    and . . . they were *very cautious* of, . .
        the group going, . .
            suddenly appear, . .
                where the enemy might be just on the other side that
                they might run into.
They always send a scout . . ahead . . to look,
    go ahead and look over the hill,

look all around, . . .
before the rest of them will go . . on their travel . . .

As they were *traveling* over hills, . .
there's a hill ahead of them, . .
and on the other side they don't know what's there,
but they *send* a scout there.
And the scout . . went up there
and he saw the enemy . . close by . . coming.
He turned around and run,
"*The enemy a coming,*
right up over the hill there,
they approaching." . . (rapid, excited voice)
Come back and told the rest of them, . .
they were back here yet
and coming to meet the enemy yet . . .

So suddenly there was a swamp, . . . (pointing with right hand)
springs I guess were nearby, . .
where water come out and run . . . from the springs, . .
woods over here . . (pointing with right hand)
They said,
"*Let's* . . *hurry* . . . *back over here* . . .
You stay *hid* . . in the woods back here, . .
and *I'll* . . . I'll meet them,
the enemy here, . .
as they come up there, . .
they're headed *right in* our direction,
they're *coming.*" . . (in a direct, commanding voice)
So . . they *rush back in,* . .
the rest of them to hide . . back there.

"*Now you wait* . . until you hear gunfire, . .
before you come out, . .
to meet the enemy.
I'll meet them, . .
single-handed, . .
without no weapon.
I'll go to this spring, . .
and I'll fix myself so they'll see me there . .

they'll find me there . . .
And I'll *gather* their weapons, . . .
    take their weapons away from them, . .
        so they'll have nothing. . . . to shoot with."
So,
    "*Alright!*" (affirming voice)
He instructed the rest of his partners,
    and they stay hid back there in the thick woods . . .

And he went rushing there,
    and took his cloths off
        he got to the mud, . .
            to those springs, . .
        and got mud all over himself, . . . (patting self all over body)
            to make him look like a *wild man*. . . .
So he went back,
    and he . . he did that.

And pretty soon here come the enemy, . . .
    up *over the hill* here they come on . .
And there they run onto the wild man, . .
    to this . . man
        who . . daubed himself with mud all over
            making him look a wild *beast* . . .
That's what the enemy think as they approached him . . .
    "*There . . there's something there*, . .
        under the spring there.
            What is it?
                Is that a *human*?
                    Kind of a *beast* of some kind!"
And . . Wise Man was crawling around,
    acting like he didn't notice them at all.
The enemy stood there and watched him. . . .
And he . . finally look up, . . .
    and he made signs,
        sign language to them . . .

He said,
    "*You must be* . . war party looking for your enemy. . . .
        I will do something for you so that you'll be successful when you

find your enemy
         that you will . . . kill off your enemy, . .
                  for you to take honors back with you." (motions with
                  hands)
This in sign language to them . . .
And that war party,
         probably . . less than ten men
                  in that enemy that . . that got to him,
                           possibly Sioux . . .
                                    could be Blackfeet.
We don't know what . . what tribe of Indians they were.
Anyway . . they were the enemy to this other group, . . .
         where Wise Man was a member of . . .
So, . . . he said those things to . . these . . Indians, . .
         standing there . . watching.

"*Alright* . . *Now*," he says, . .
         "*Give me* your rifles, . . .
                  I'll put them over here . . .
         "I'll *put medicine* onto your rifles and everything, (patting hands
         together)
                  so you'll be *successful* when you *use them* in killing your . .
                  enemy." . .
"Oh, *oh*, oh, *oh*!
         alright, . .
                  let's hand him our . . . guns." . .
They got off and they . . brought them.
"Stack them up right here." (pointing with right hand)
And they set them up over here. (continues pointing)

Now they're without weapons.
"*Now* I'll say prayers for you . . .
         I'll . . fix each of your . . your rifles,
                  put medicine to them."
He looks them over,
         sees that there is shells in them.
Work on one rifle, . .
         take another one, . . .
                  do that, . . .

and his partners were watching, . . .
                right there watching, . .
                        all ready to approach, . .
                                when the time comes . . .
He did that, . .
        and . . looked . . at these enemies' rifles over . . .
Put a shell into . . into one of them, . .
        points them around. . . . .
And he point at the enemy, . .
        and they stood there.
"*He's making* medicine for us,
        he's fixing up our rifles.
                So we're going to be successful with them, . .
                        when he gets *through with* them,
                                gives back our . . rifles
                                        and we'll go on." . .
He stood there,
        they all stood there on their horses watching him . . .

And he points. . . . at things . . , (pointing off)
        finally point at one of them, . .
                with a *shell* in it
                        and *pulled the trigger* (clapped hands)
                                and that *one*, . .
                                        the *gun* fire . . .
As he instructed his partners
        "When you *hear* a gunshot, . .
                you *come approaching*." . . . (assertive voice)
They *waited* for that,
        and when they heard the gunshot,
                they'd been *watching* him anyway . . .
He pointed at one of them, (pointing off)
        shot
                and . . killed that one right now that shot . . . (hit hands together)

Then the enemy,
        his partners . . . *come out* of there,
                "*Ahhhhhhh*" (war cry, clapping hands, excited)
They're over here,

their guns over here,
    they have *nothing* . . .
Enemy came
    and they . . they got all of them. . . . (patting hands together)
They *kill* all of them . . .

So . . Wise Man has *all their rifles*, . .
    and they scalp all of them . .
Wise Man kill one,
    and the others . . got the rest.
For they have nothing to fight with,
    their guns over here.
They were in *turmoil*,
    not knowing what to do.
They came and they got all of them, . . (patting hands together)
    kill them all right there, . .
        scalped them, . .
            count coups, . .
              got their guns
                and everything.
They went with great honors back to their camp.
And that's what was accomplished by Wise Man. . . . (in a proud voice)

BURNT FACE
PLENTY HAWK, CROW[23]

There is a boy who falls into a fire while playing,
    burns his face.
He grows up to be a man,
    but does not like his face,
        always stays inside his lodge.
Whenever he goes out he first paints his face.
The other side of his face is very good-looking.[24]

One day this young man tells his mother to make plenty of moccasins.
He wishes to go away,
    but his mother would not let him.
However, his father supports him,
    tells his wife to make the moccasins.

So she makes them,
      gives them to the boy.

He makes a tipi among the pines.
The next day he goes off for a vision.
In the tipi he has meat and moccasins hanging from the poles.
After awhile he comes back to his tipi.

The next day he goes out again.
This time they talk to him.
Someone asks,
      "What are you doing here?
            Why have you broken my tipi poles?"
The young man says,
"I hate something very much,
      that is why I have come here."
"Go back to your tipi,
      return next morning."

He goes,
      stays there overnight,
            returns to the place early in the morning.
He sees a big white tipi there.
They call him in;
      he looks around,
            everywhere he sees all kinds of medicine tied to curtain strings.
"Pick out one medicine."
"I don't want any,
      but I hate something very much."
"What is it?"
"I hate one side of my face."
"I can do nothing for you,
      go on farther to the mountains."
He tells him just where to go.

He goes on to the next place.
It is a considerable distance,
      he sleeps several times on the way.

He gets there,

Tipi poles at
Crow Fair.

      fixes up a little tipi.
Inside he takes a stick,
      hangs up his belongings again.

The next morning he goes out to the place.
After two days there is a tipi there.
They call him in.
"What are you trying for?"
"I hate something very much,
      that is why I am here."
"What is it?"
"One side of my face."
"Go on still farther."
He shows him just where to go.

He goes back to his tipi,

stays there overnight,
    then he goes on.
He arrives at the third place.
Below a high hill he puts up a strong tipi,
    in it he puts a pole across,
        has his belongings there.
He stays there overnight,
    then he goes to a high hill for a few days.

He sees an Eagle high in the air circling about.
He sees it come down.
The Eagle comes,
    sits by the man.
"What are you crying over?"
"I hate one side of my face,
    that is why."
"Go back to your tipi,
    stay there.
    Tomorrow I'll come there,
        see you,
            tell you some things."

The young man goes back to his tipi,
    stays there overnight.
Next morning he waits for the Eagle to come.
He goes and lays down in his tipi.

After awhile he hears a noise like that made by a strong wind.
A person comes,
    sits by the tipi,
        enters,
            talks to him.
"I'll help you but you will have to help me.
    On the other side of the hill where you had a vision
        there is a big lake,
            in the middle there is an island with a nest in it.
    Whenever I have children something comes up out of the lake,
        eats up my little ones.
I ask you to help me."
The young man says,

"I will help you."

The Eagle takes the man to the lake.
There he shows him where to go on further,
    the Eagle is to meet him there.
The Eagle's nest holds two eggs.

He starts to the place.
In the first coulee there is nice clean water,
    a path runs by the creek.
He goes on,
    thinks of getting a drink from the creek.
When he goes to do so he hears a spirit say,
    "Don't drink of that water,"
        so he jumps across.

After awhile he sees a Bear lying down there.
He stops in front of the Bear,
    he cries.
The Bear says,
    "I have been waiting for you to come.
        Get on my back."
He gets on his back,
    they start off toward the place the Eagle had shown him.

They get there.
There is a big hill,
    at the top he lets the young man off.
The Bear goes away,
    the young man goes uphill.

He goes up where the Eagle had shown him.
    The Eagle is there.
He asks the young man,
    "How did you get here so soon?"
Someone brought me here."
"Who?"
"The Bear."
"That Bear is very dangerous.
    'When the Sun comes by,

he will say something to you,
    you'll do what he says.
I'll wash you so you can talk to the Sun."

The Eagle starts off in the air.
He makes medicine,
    causes rain to fall upon the young man.
No clouds are to be seen,
    but the Eagle made rain.

After washing him he comes down again,
    tells him to go to the same place,
        to the lake and the hill of his vision.
"You'll wait for me if you get there first,
    I'll wait for you if I get there sooner."
The Eagle goes up into the air again,
    goes to his nest.

The young man goes down from the hill.
Halfway down he makes a tipi,
    puts in his things.
He stays there overnight.

The next morning he goes up early on the high hill.
A Little Bird comes up,
    says to the young man,
        "Say to the Sun,
            'You love your son,'
        then tell him your troubles."

He stays on the hill 'til evening,
    when sunset comes the Sun turns round to the young man saying,
        "You'll run four times,
            then you'll reach my place."

He goes right on.
While he is on the hill the Little Bird comes again, saying,
    "They are waiting for you on the riverside."

The young man goes to the river.

He goes to the place.
Four Ducks are there awaiting him,
    their heads are blue.
One of them says,
    "Get on my back,
        do not open your eyes till I tell you."
He gets on the back,
    they set out.

They come to a piece of ground,
    on the island he tells him to open his eyes.
Then he sees nothing but water all over as far as he can see.
They stopped.
After awhile four black Ducks come.
Then the other Ducks go back to where the man started.
One black Duck tells him to shut his eyes,
    get on his back.
He starts off with him.

After a long time they stop,
    the Bird tells him to open his eyes.
He is on another island with nothing but water around about.
The Ducks sit,
    talk with him awhile,
        four white Ducks come,
            the black Ducks depart.

One white Duck says,
    "Get on my back,
        do not open your eyes till I tell you."
They start off again.

They stop,
    he is told to open his eyes.
Far off he sees some land.
After they had talked with him,
    four spotted Ducks come,
        one of them says,
            "Come ride on my back."
The young man gets on his back, }

Duck near the Gallatin River in southwestern Montana.

shuts his eyes.

After awhile they stop.
The Duck tells him to open his eyes.
They are setting in the shore of a big sea,
    he sees a little boy and girl playing by it.
The young man goes up to them,
    they run away.
As soon as he had gotten off the Ducks, he approached the children,
    they run to their mother, saying,
        "We have found a brother."

He follows them.
The little girl tells her mother she had seen a poor person,
    the boy says he wants to come in.
At the door are two dogs,
    one is a Bear,
        the other a Mountain Lion.
As he comes in,
    these dogs growl as if to jump on the man,
        but the woman inside scolds them,
            both cease.

He comes inside.
She gives him some food to eat.
For awhile the little boy sits on the young man's lap.
The boy says,

"Make me a bow and arrows."
The girl,
  "Brother, make me a ball and shinny stick."
The young man goes out,
  cuts cherry trees,
    makes a shinny stick first for the little girl
      then bow and arrows for the little boy.

When the little boy comes back from playing,
  the man tells him he has no feathers.
The boy and girl go out to get feathers.
They come back,
  have none.
After awhile someone comes,
  throws in feathers for them.

He took them,
  fixes the feathers for them.
He fixes arrows,
  shows them how to use them.

He has already made a shinny stick for the girl,
  he also wants to make a ball but needs some antelope hair.
She asks her mother if she has any.
"No, but I have seen some that someone has sheared off."
The children go out,
  bring them in,
    then he makes a ball for the little girl.
The next day he shows them how to play shinny.

After awhile the boy asks,
  "Why have you come here?"
"I have a bad face,
  that is why I have come here."
The little boy says,
  "My father has a looking glass,
    I'll bring it,
      let you use it."
The girl hears it too,

goes inside,
      gets the looking glass.

The young man uses it,
      sees himself in it.
His face is as good as when he was first born.
After he uses the looking glass his face is perfect,
      he is glad.

When the Sun comes back to his tipi,
      he tells his family what he has seen on his trip.
He asks the young man if he wants to wait twenty or forty days.
The young man says he will wait twenty days.

After twenty days he is asked whether he wants to go home.
"Before you leave,
      wash your face in the spring,
            then when you get home and see the Sun,
                  don't make faces but look straight into my face."
As he started off,
      the little children cried because he is going away.[25]

This young man leaves,
      starts on the Duck's back.
He comes home as he had gone the other way.

After he gets across he goes up to the hill again.
The Eagle is waiting for him there.
They talk awhile.
He goes to his tipi,
      gets his things,
            goes on to the lake.

The Eagle carries the man across the island in the middle of the lake.
The Eagle says,
      "Four times it will get foggy in the afternoon and morning,
            the fourth time an animal will come out of the water."
"Go and pack all the wood you can."
The Eagle brings him plenty of wood.

The young man takes four big stones,
    has them ready as if for a sweat-bathing.

He waits.
A big fog rises early in the morning,
    in the afternoon,
        just before dark,
            it is foggy again.
As soon as the fog had all lifted an animal comes out,
    opening its mouth wide as it is coming up the steep hill.
The young man takes a stick,
    throws a hot stone into its mouth.
A second time he throws one in.
A third time he does it again.
Then the monster stops.
He throws in the fourth stone,
    the animal goes back into the water.

The Eagle is up in the air,
    whistling in the meantime,
        not knowing what to do.
When he sees the animal go back into the water,
    the Eagle is happy,
        comes down.

As soon as this animal dies,
    it floats up,
        goes round and round the island,
            which it completely surrounds.
They see it die,
    it is the Long Otter.
        The Thunder comes now,
            takes the Long Otter,
                goes away with him.

The Eagle tells the young man to wait for his brother and sister,
    the young Eagles he has saved.
"When they are grown up,
    they will take you home."
He builds a tipi,

has plenty to eat,
    is always happy.

He waits 'til one day the Sun comes close,
    tells the Eagle,
        "The young man's father and mother have suffered for a long
        time.
            You must send him home as soon as you can."
He goes right in,
    the Eagle tells the young man,
        "At the first snowfall I'll send you home.
            Your brother will take you."

The little birds are grown up,
    practice flying.
At the first snowfall the man goes on his brother's back while his sister car-
ries his belongings,
    thus they take him home.
Before starting, the Eagle gives him medicine,
    "Whenever you have a big tipi make the picture of an Eagle on it."
He takes an eagle's claw beaded on each side,
    gives it to the young man for a necklace,
        also an eagle foot.

He starts homeward on the young Eagle's back.
They come over the mountains down to the man's home.
From the air they see two persons seated on a high hill.
The Eagles see them,
    tell him,
        "There are your father and your mother."

They come up.
His father and mother hear the sound.
The Birds are coming to them.
They get to the ground.
The young man gets off.
The father turns around,
    sees his son.
He jumps up,
    puts his arm around his neck,

is very glad.
He sees that their son has a good face.
Just before the Eagles leave,
    they tell the young man to kill a buffalo,
        open its belly,
            leave it there.

The parents go home with their son,
    the Eagles turn back.
The next morning they chase,
    kill a buffalo,
        cut it open,
            go home.

After a few days he gets married.
A pretty girl had said,
    "If he did not have a bad face,
        I should take him for my sweetheart."
Someone told him this,
    that is why he went to seek a vision.
Now he marries this girl.

After he gets married he makes a big tipi,
    spreads it out flat,
        calls men to draw and paint eagles on it.
He tells the men,
    "When you have done the picture,
        I'll know what is going to happen."
After the tipi is put up,
    he could foretell what kind of a day,
        what kind of storm they are going to have.

|

BURNT FACE
TOM YELLOWTAIL, CROW[26]

In the days when they *still* . . move about the country, . .
    the territory where the Crow Indians . . roam . . about,
        moving from one place to another,
            is this area . . . comprising . . the rivers, . .

                    the Little Bighorn, . .
                        the Bighorn, . .
                            the Yellowstone River, . .
                                and the Missouri River . . .
And the Indians . . would follow some of these rivers, . .
        move about every few days, . .
            from way down there next to the North Dakota border . . line, . .
                on up this way toward these Bighorn Mountains. (points to
                east, then to south)
And even beyond the mountains,
        and they'd go . . over the mountains
            on over to the *next* mountains,
                which is the Rocky Mountains,
                    where . . the present . . town of . . Cody is now
                    located.
They'd go that far
        and then they'd return
            and come back . . . back along the Yellowstone,
                and follow that on down, . .
                    possibly as far. . . . to the North Dakota border . . .
And they'd turn around,
        and come back.
And *those* . . those are the areas they roam about,
        just south of us to . .
            all the way down to . . almost Cheyenne, Wyoming.
It's a wide area where they'd roam about . . .

And . . this one time this group, . .
        I would imagine it, . .
            could be the Mountain Crow . . . group,[27]
                that had went down almost as far as the North Dakota . .
                border (points east)
                    and then return and camp,
                        coming back to the Bighorn Mountain.
                        (points south)
They don't *move* . . very far every time they move,
        they only *move* about ten miles, . .
            and *make* a new encampment, . .
                they don't travel very far, . .
                    for they travel slow.

Bighorn River in
Montana.

Camp a few days,
  wherever they camp,
    they spend a few days
      and then continue on . .

As they were moving up the,
  I would say possibly the Bighorn Valley, . . .
    on up . . .
And in the evening, . .
  in the camp
    the children . . would *play*,
      build a bonfire
        or something like that
    and played . . .
And this one night they did build a bonfire, . .
  and they were chasing each other around, playing games . . .
And a young lad of about . . the age of this boy here now. (pointing to one of
his great-grandsons in the room)
I'd say the lad was probably was about ten years old.
They were all *playing* around this bonfire,
  chasing each other.
And while they were playing like that
  chasing each other,
    some were . . standing back
      and others would be chasing around each other,
  and *somebody*. . . . gave a *push* to this one boy as he was going,
    the fire over here. (pointing to floor to right)
And when he got *pushed*,
  he fell into that . . into that bonfire

which burned him pretty bad . . before they rescued him,
    pulled him out, . .
        but he was *burned* already . . pretty bad, . .
           into the bonfire, . .
             the *big* fire he fell into . . . (placing hands
             over face)

And . . . that accident happened
    so that . . . the other children all quit playing, . .
        for one of them got hurt.
And . . . the *child* was taken to his camp,
    his parents' camp.
And they took care of him.
And the next few days . . . the *sores* started coming out (from) that burn, . .
    on his face. (hands to face)
And he was *burned* so . . so much that . . his face had to . . sores were on
    and finally come to . . to heal as *scabs* . . .
And . . he would still try to play with his other friends . . . yet . . .
    but his face was disfigured then
        after these . . soars had healed
           and . . tightened up (hands still close to face)
             and his face was . . disfigured . .
And . . the other kids would make *fun* of him,
    "*Ahh,* look at him, (pointing)
        look at his *funny* . . *ugly* face!"
    And all that
And that made the boy. . . . . ashamed. (low, saddened voice)
He felt ashamed the way the other kids would make fun of him . . .
    an ugly face . . . (hands to face)

So . . he didn't like that
    and he wanted to leave camp
        be away from . . staying in camp.
So . . he . . got bedding,
    and . . things to stay away from the camp.
When the camp move about,
    he'd travel along the side of them,
        I'd say probably a half a mile away from them or so . . .
And he doesn't come into camp

for he was ashamed . . of what the other kids would make fun of
him, . .
    when they look at him . . .

So he stayed that way . .
    and . . his parents would try to bring him back
      and he won't do it . . .
He has his bedding . . .
And he stays there
    and they bring food for him . . .
And he's sad
    and he doesn't come back into the camp, . .
      to play with the other, . .
        his friends, . .
          other children.

And as the camp *move about,*
    moving south . . from way down . . . the Dakota lines, . .
      move about . . up the . . the Missouri River (pointing north)
      and then they branch off.
And they . . they followed the Bighorns, . .
    move about,
      moving toward the Bighorn Mountains . . (look to north)
And he . . he had in mind,
    as they were . . approaching the Bighorn Mountains, . .
    he thought to himself, . .
      "*Now* . . when we get to this . . Bighorn Mountains, . .
        I'll . . I'll quit staying alone, . .
          with my people, . .
            with my parents.
              My parents are among . . the group
              in that camp.
      I'll leave them when we get to these mountains,
        and *take* the mountains,
          and go up somewhere
           and *fast*." . .
So . . he told his parents . . to make him . . several pairs of moccasins
and to prepare when the men go . . hunting
    and making jerky, (patting fists together)
      to save up . . . plenty of jerky, . .

to take with him when he leaves, . .
       when they get to the mountains,
    and quite a few pairs of extra pairs of moccasins, . .
    and enough . . enough clothing, . .
      to leave . . to leave the camp.
The camp could go on
    and he'd take to the mountains, . .
    and fast somewhere. . .
"I'll go do that,
    if I return, . .
      if I'm lucky through my fasting
        and I . . may return to my people.
If not,
    if something happens to me,
      that'll . . that'll be it,
        that'll be alright." . . (hands raised slightly)
He knew those conditions,
    but he decided he's going to . . leave the camp,
      they can go on,
    and he would . . . he would leave the camp
      and take the mountains
        and fast somewhere.
So . . the parents prepared all those pairs of extra moccasins for him, (patting
fists together)
    things he would need for him to get along with,
      extra cloths, . . (points hands to self)
        and the jerky, . .
          for his food, . .
    so he could spend quite a few days, . .
      quite awhile, . .
        before he . . would return to his people.
He wanted to do that fasting.
So . . alright. . . . . he was determined to do that fasting . .

So they got to the mountains
    and he bid his folks goodbye for awhile, . .
      other friends.
"Now you folks go on
    and I'll . . I'll take these mountains
      and I'll . . I'll find a place where I'll fast, . .

for quite awhile." . .
So *the camp* went on
And he took to the mountains
over here . . possibly over here, . .
into the canyon where Fort Smith is now, . .
probably left . . there.
And the camp went through the canyon (motions with hands)
and on over to the other side, . .
moving towards, . .
into Wyoming
towards . . that area
on the other side of the mountains
around Cody, Wyoming, area.
That's where they were headed . . .

So he left the camp
and he took the mountains
and went south, . .
along the mountain range . . .
Kept on . . traveling, . . .
on south, . .
into Wyoming . . .
Kept traveling south until . . finally he come to a place,
"*I believe this* is a good place," . .
where the present Medicine Wheel is now. (confident)
He come to that place, . .
look things over . . the country, . .
"Right here is where I will . . . fast!" . .

So he did,
he started fasting there, . .
right where the Medicine . . Wheel is now . . .
He fasted there (points with hand)
and *during the day,* . .
where he fasted . . .
a lot of the place is just rocky . . formations of rocks, . .
all around him . .
So during the day he would gather . . . he would gather rocks.
And he started forming . . a *circle,* . .
representing . . the lodge, . .

the lodge you seen nowadays
      that comprise . . the *Sun Dance* Lodge.
He *built* . . . the large circle, (circling motion with hands)
    everyday he'd pile up rocks on top of
          to form a circle,
                and the *doorway* toward the rising Sun
                      to the east.
He made it *big* . . (hands opened)
And everyday he works, . .
      and the spokes that lead to the center. . . .
            he piles up rocks leading to the center . . .
What you see now . . on a . . Sun Dance Lodge, . .
      it is round, . .
            with a doorway leading towards the Sun, . .
                  to the east where the Sun rises.
And *he built that* according to . . the form of a Sun Dance Lodge, . .
      built it according to the Sun Dance Lodge . . . [28]

And . . . no telling how many, . .
      he must of stayed there a month or so . . .
And he fasted . . fasted there.
Everyday he says his prayers, . .
      he has his tobacco . . with him, . .
            a good supply of tobacco.
And he'd fill up his pipe, (motions as if filling a pipe)
      and offer smokes . . to the Great Spirit . .
And . . he went that way on all these days of fasting . . .

And . . . right by is the *cliffs*, . .
      caves, . .
            where . . you hear about the Little People. (looks out to the
            distance)
They are *there*,
      and *they're there yet today* . . .

Finally . . the Little People come out,
      they'd been *watching* him . . .
They come out, . .
      and they . . they said,
            "Young man, . .
                  you have been here for awhile

Crow Sun Dance
lodge, 1993.

we've been watching you.
You're fasting,
    you've said your prayers,
        and you've spent enough time here, . .
            and you've built this, . .
                representing a Sun Dance Lodge.
It is good . . (motions with hand)
Now we want to ask you,
    we want to adopt you,
        we want to give you medicine.
We want you *to quit your fasting*
    and you go back to your people . .
Your people are . . at that place, (pointing off)
    your parents and the rest of them . . .
Now you go back to that place
    and you will come to your people.
Your *parents* are there . . .
You get back . . back to your people,
    don't stay away from them.
We'll take those scars away from you
    so you'll look . . look decent,
        so you won't be ashamed to get back into your people
        . . .
And . . the *medicine things* we will give you . . you will have them . . .
And. . . . you pray for people, . .

doctor people, . .
>when you are back home you'll have that power we
>have given you. (closed fists gently hit one
>another)
We are *giving you* . . all these *powers.*
So . . you exercise, . .
>using your medicines when you get back to your people.
The *children,* . .
>your *friends,* . .
>>if they make fun of you will quit.
They will *respect you,*
>for you're going to be having . . *medicine* . . *things*
>>that they will have to respect you.
And . . you will be a medicine man among your people
>and eventually become a *chief* . . of your tribe." . .
"*So. . . . alright* . . I will leave, . .
>I'll go back." . .

So he started back the way he came,
>and went to the place where the Little People had told him where he
>will find his people,
>>probably several days to travel,
>>>he's afoot . . .
And . . he went to the place where they told, . .
>the Little People . . told him, . .
>>where he would find his people.
And he *traveled* and *traveled* to that place,
>and sure enough . . *there's* the camp.
His parents are there, (points with hand)
>his people he'd *left,*
>>when they got to the . . to the Bighorn Mountains when he left
>>them. (points south)
And he was gone *so long* . . that people begin to think . . . something must of
happened,
>"Look like he's not going to return." . .
Some . . had mourn over him,
>start mourning . . over him.

So one day . . here he come into camp.
He asked for the chief's camp,

and they . . they told him
"There's the chief's camp."
He went there to the chief's, . .
the present chief of the camp . . .
And he told them.
The chief looked at him,
he's grown up already,
he was a young lad when he left them,
he's a young man now
and he didn't recognize him.
So the young man . . . explained to the chief,
"I am the boy who left the camp down there.
I'm the boy that got his face burned,
and I stayed away from the camp.
And I'm . . I'm the boy.
I've grown up now.
I've fasted . . like I wanted to.
I received my medicine. (makes fists with hands)
And *here* . . I was asked to return to my people
and here I am.
I've come back
My parents are here somewhere."
So the chief said,
"*Okay, alright,* (claps hands together once)
come on in." . .

And he calls an announcer,
a herald we call them,
the man who goes around camp making announcements . . .
The chief called the herald . . to come
and he told him the story.
"Go around the camp
and tell the different chiefs to come,
get together
and come to my camp.
And we'll have a smoke.
We have *this young man* who has returned to us.
We will hear his story.
We will ask him to tell his story to us." . .
So the herald went around camp,

"*All you chiefs,* . .
        now in camp, . .
                proceed over to . . the main chief's, . .
                        the head chief's camp.
There's a young man that's returned to us, . .
        a member of our group here, . .
                of our tribe, . .
                        that has returned to us.
We will hear his story.
Report to the chief's, . .
        the head chief's camp.
Then we'll hear this young man's story"
So . . after they heard that
        the different chiefs in the camp . . . went to the head chief's camp . . .

And there, . .
        its *a big tipi,* . .
                and there . . they come in. (points)
The chief sits here (points with hands to right)
        and they have the boy there. (points to left)
They came
        and take their places.
And they . . they have the ceremony, . .
        they . . they filled up their pipes (motions, filling a pipe)
                and smoke, . .
                        make incense, . .
                                prayers . . . (hands opened)

And after *doing* that they say
        "*Alright,* young man, . .
                we are now *ready* to hear your story.
        Tell us, . .
                where you had been, . .
                        when you left us
                and all that.
        We want to hear that.
        All these chiefs are ready to hear you." . .
So . . the young man . . says,
        "*I am the boy,* . .
                that when, . .

quite awhile back
            when we were . . moving up from *way down* there, . .
                way down the Missouri, . .
                        headed this way up the Bighorn . .
                        River, . .
        when we got to the mountain
            were I left . . you people, . .
                    and I . . I went to the mountains
            and I went on south from there, . .
                    quite aways down
            and come to a place where I fasted
                    and stayed in one place.
I spent . . all my time there.
And finally . . *the Little People* there were around close by
        come to me,
                and . . visit with me,
                    and *talk* with me.
And they advise me to leave that place
        and come back to . . back to my parents
                and all of you, . .
                        and I'm a *member* of your group . .
And according to what I received
        they call me,
                Burnt Face,
                        and I was disfigured.
But those . . Little People took those . . took those . . disfiguration off of
my face
        and make me look different.
So *here I am.*
        I'm the boy who left your camp."
"*Ahhh, ahhh, ahh, hay*!
    That's great!".
            the chief said.
"*Alright,* . .
        we will . . welcome you back to our camp.
    You will be with us now . . .
    Stay with us.
    We'll travel on." . .

So . . they accepted him back . .

Sweet man-sage near
Wyola, Montana.

They announce, . .
    throughout the camp.
        "The *young man* is back with us,
            he is back to his parents.
        He is with us now from now on.
        We will *depend* on him
        When . . some of you get sick you call on him.
        He's been given the *power* to work
            and doctor you (closed fists gently hit one another)
                and make you get well.
        He'll be the *man* we call on, . .
            as our *doctor*, . .
                among this group." . .

So . . sure enough . . camp went on, . .
　　　people . . *respect him* . . .
Anyone that get sick they would call on him, . .
　　　and he'd pray for them,
　　　　　doctor them
　　　　　　　and they'd get well . .
And they respect him,
　　　"*Oh,* this man has the power
　　　　　We must respect him
　　　　　　　We can't make fun of him no more, . .
　　　　　　　　　no way, . .
　　　　　　　　　　　anymore."
So as time went on he finally become a chief, . .
　　　and a *great chief* from that time on . . (hands opened)
And his name was . . Burnt Face . . . 29

I

THE LITTLE PEOPLE
TOM YELLOWTAIL, CROW[30]

We talk about the Little People, . . .
　　　that are among the mountains, . .
　　　　　in fact . . . my own medicine . . come from the . . Little People that
　　　　　I call on. . . .
And . . this one time, . .
　　　not too long ago, . .
　　　　　possibly I would say . . about fifteen years ago when this hap-
　　　　　pened, . .
　　　on our present day . . buffalo pasture
　　　　　on . . the south of the Bighorn Canyon, . .
　　　　　　　what they call the Yellowtail Dam, . . .
　　　　　　　　　branches of canyons that run into the . . main Big-
　　　　　　　　　horn Canyon are the Black Canyon, . . (points)
　　　　　　　　　　　the Bull Elk Canyon. , (points)
　　　　　　　　　　　　　and so forth that lead into it.
And in that area is, . .
　　　where our buffalo pasture is . . *now,* . .
　　　　　comprising a big area, . .
　　　　　　　of some near thirty thousand acres, . .
　　　there where our tribal buffalo herds . . are being kept.

They have natural . . canyons that comprise *high walls*, (motions with hands
to sky)
>   that *not* . . *not very much* fencing has been done to close up this . . wide
>   space
>>   comprising around twenty-five to thirty thousand acres, . .
>>   where our tribal herd of buffalo are being kept *today* . . .

And . . some fifteen years ago . . the buffalo warden, . .
>   a man, . . .
>>   a clan brother of mine, . . [31]
>>>   who comes to visit me, . .
>>>>   josh with me, . .
>>>>>   because that's our . . general . . custom,
>>>>>>   according to our Indian ways,
>>>>>   that we josh each other, . .
>>>>>>   whenever we meet. ,
>>>>>>>   not meaning anything *real*
>>>>>   but we josh, . .
>>>>>>   make jokes, . .
>>>>>>   and so forth.
And . . . this . . buffalo warden at that time who is Frank . . He Does It, . .
>   who *lives* . . in the Bighorn valley,
>>   his home is in the Bighorn valley,
>>>   close to . . the present-day . . Fort Smith. . . .
And . . he had this job of being the buffalo warden,
>   so he *stays up there* . .
There is a cabin up there
>   which we call "hunter's cabin." . .
And it's a place provided by the . . tribe, . .
>   for the buffalo warden to live in, . .
>>   it's a . . log cabin,
>>>   a barn,
>>>>   corrals,
>>>>>   a good spring close by . . .
And . . the areas . . for camping is very . . nice
>   around near that . . cabin
>>   where the buffalo warden stays . . .
And he stays up there,
>   has his saddle horses to ride around with, . .
>>   looking over the buffalo herds, . .

check the . . fence lines,
      and so forth . . .
And he lives and stays there. .
   all alone . . .

And . . *this* . . *one night,*
   when he rode during the day
      and come back and put his horse away, . .
         in the barn, . .
            corral, . .
               for the night, . .
   he retired, . .
      nightfall had come . . .
He come into his cabin,
   and prepared himself a little . . supper . . .
And . . after he ate, . .
   had his supper, . .
      he laid down on his bed,
         had his lights . . his lights on,
           and . . reading magazines, . .
              old newspapers,
               and so forth.
He was laying on his bed, . .
   all alone, . . .
      he's batching it up there
   he's all alone, . . .
      nobody near . . .
And while he's . . laying there, . .
   silent,
      reading . . by his . . lights . . .
And . . all at once he heard a *little noise*?. (questioning and looking off to his porch)
   out on his porch,
      porch like this that's out here . . (pointing to his own porch to his left)
He heard a *little noise* . . out there, . .
   thinking
      "*Somebody's* coming?" (whispering)
He's listen! (whispering)

Pretty soon . . . there is a *knock* on his door, . . (patting hands together)
    a *knock* . . . on his door . .
And he says,
    "*Hay, hay, come on in,* (loud, welcoming voice)
        come in!" (motions with hand to come in)
The door opened, . .
    and in walked *four little men,* . . . (holds out four fingers)
        standing about three and a half . . four feet . . . *high,*
            that's . . the height of the Little People, . .
    a grown man, . .
        he maybe a hundred-year-old man, . .
            only . . standing about three and a half feet high
                or so, . .
    Little People just like a little . . a little . . tiny child, . .
        is what they are, . .
            that's the size of them.
Yet . . they are powerful, . . .
    the strength of a giant, . . (strong voice)
        is what those Little People, . .
            as *little as they are.* . . . .
They have the *medicine,* . .
    they have the *strength,* . .
        so they take care of things . . .
But . . . they come to the buffalo warden to do them a favor . . .

So Frank sit up on his bed, . .
    put his reading magazine away . . .
He says,
    "*Well,* . . *what can I do for you?.* . .
        You must come to see me about something." . .
"Yes, . .
    we come to ask you to do a favor, . .
        and we'd like to have you do this tomorrow morning . . .
    We live down here, . .
        in . . the canyon, .
            under the cliffs, . .
                the caves, .
                    is where we live . . .
    Our group are . . needing some meat, . .

we're getting short on meat.
And we come to ask you to get a . . *buck deer* for us tomorrow morning . .
Drag him down over to the high cliff above where we live,
    where we are . .
Get him there, . .
    and drop him down over the cliff,
        down to us . . .
And we'll take care of the . . of the meat, . .
    when *you do* get this big buck . . .
Now tomorrow morning . . . you get up early, . .
    saddle up your horse (patting hands together)
        and *go down* . . down this trail toward the canyon, . .
            there's . . heavy timber there
        and that trail will lead you into an open spaces like that,
        (points with hand)
            and another one,
                and so on, . .
        going on down toward the canyon." . .
The canyon is about a mile away to the cliff, . .
    from where he lives, . .
        where the cabin is, . .
        where he is staying. . . .
"*So,* in the morning when you saddle up (motions with hands)
    and take your rifle,
        and . . rope,
            and things along with you
                your gun, . .
    and you *take the trail* . . this trail,
        and you come to one of those openings,
            there will stand . . a *big buck deer,* . . .
                stand there . . looking at you,
    and you get off
        and shoot . . . (pats hands together once)
Get him for us . .
After you get him
    put your rope around him,
        drag him down to the cliff,
            drag him on down beyond the high cliff, . .
        and drop him down . .
We'll take care of that after you do that for us . . .

That's what we've come to see you about tonight, . .
                    to ask you to do this favor for us." . . .
So Frank says
        "Alright, very well,
                I will do that for you.
        If you are out of meat,
                and need meat, . .
                        I'll . . get that buck for you like you say, . .
                                bring it down there
                                        and drop it down, . .
        and you'll have meat." . .
"Alright, okay,
        that's what we come to see you about.
        Now we will go . . .
        And we thank you very much for your favor to do this,
                that will give our people some meat.
        We are out of meat
                and that's why we've come to ask you to this . . favor for us . .
        So-o, . . alright Frank,
                now we'll go"
And they turn around . . towards the door
        and away they went, . .
                dark out there. . . .

So Frank got to think,
        "Well, in order to get up early, . .
                to do that for these Little People, . .
                        I must go to bed now, (looks down at own watch)
                                I'll quit reading." . .
And he got ready
        and went to bed.
Set his timer to get up early, . .
        alarm clock,
                to get up early,
                        before . . before daylight . . .
So he went to bed.
He quit reading,
        and put his lights out
                and took . . his sleep, (claps hands once)
                        and got up early . . the next morning . . .

The alarm clock rang
  and he jumped up, . . (claps hands once)
    and . . he hit the coffee a little bit,
      and he took that (claps hands once)
  and went out
    and saddled up, . . (motions with hands)
  took his rifle out
    shells, . .
      his rope on the saddle . . .
Saddled up
  and got on him . . on his horse, . .
    and . . started taking that trail . . .
Come to that opening,
  sure enough
    there stood that *five point bi-i-g . . buck deer,*
      looking at him.
"*The-e-re's what* they said I would come to."
He got off.
The deer just stood there, . .
  just look at him like a statue . . .
He got off
  took his time
    took his rifle out. . . .
(claps hands loudly)
Shoot,
  and down went the . . the big buck. . . .
So he got on his horse
  and went over to it.
Took his knife out,
  bleed it . . .
Great big . . ni-i-ce big buck,
  five point . . .
Took his rope off (motions with hands)
  and put it on the horns,
    put it on the saddle horn . . .
Drug that deer, . .
  on that trail on, . .
    on over to the cliff . . .
"This is the cliff.
  Here is the cliff where they asked me to . . to push the deer off on . .

over the cliff, . .
　　down to them." . .
He drug the deer right on top close by
　　and he got off
　　　　and he tied his horse . . .
And he says,
　　"Now Little People, . .
　　　　here is the deer you asked me . . to get for you this morning.
　　　　　　I got him
　　　　　　　　and I *brought* him,
　　　　　　　　　　and here it is . .
　　I'm going to *drop* him on downover this cliff to you . . .
　　Then you take care of him like you say you will."
After he said those prayers, . . .
　　he pushed . . . the deer on over to the dropoff, . .
　　　　pushed him on over . . .
The deer went down
　　possibly a hundred-feet-high . . cliff.
He watched it, . .
　　and it hit down there
　　　　and it rolled . . a little ways, . .
　　　　　　pine trees growing like that, (holds fingers up)
　　　　　　　　he rolled . . a little ways,
　　　　　　　　　　rolled up against a standing pine tree. . . .
(claps hands loudly)
Stopped,
　　and there it was . .
"*Okay,*
　　they should take care of it,
　　　　that's just the way they want it
　　　　　　and there it is."
He turned around
　　and got on his horse
　　　　and come back . . . come back home to cook his breakfast
　　　　　　after he had done this favor . .
　　　　　　　　for the Little People.
Got himself breakfast,
　　ate,
　　　　and then he went about his . . *chores,*
　　　　　　looking over the buffalo . . .

That kept in his mind . . .
The *next day,* . . .
　　"I must go
　　　　and see . . .
　　It's staying in my mind.
　　I'll go
　　　　and see . . . if that . . that deer is still there yet
　　　　　　or gone?"

So he . . went back down there, . .
　　looked down where . . he'd . . dropped the deer down over the cliff.
And *it's gone down there.* . . . .
Soon as he did that I imagine they were waiting for him,
　　they must of . . took him,
　　　　took care of it.
So the deer was gone.

And he did that *favor* . . for the Little People, . .
　　of the mountains . . .
And there's a . . big colony of them . . in our Black Canyon . . .
They're there. . . . .

LITTLE HEAD
TOM YELLOWTAIL, CROW[32]

In the days . . . before we were settled, . .
　　roaming around this country, . . .
　　　　war parties would go from one tribe against . . their enemies, . .
　　　　　　to the other tribes that were roaming around also in this
　　　　　　area . . . (a very slow and deliberate voice)
Wherever they *meet,*
　　they sometimes get to meet
　　　　and a *battle* would take place.
They would have *wa-a-r* . . .
Fighting would take place . . .

This man whose name is . . Little Head, . . .
　　is a Crow . . . warrior, . .

in his younger days. (continues in a very slow and deliberate
   voice)
And *he*
   and a . . friend of his,
      just the two of them got . . out
         and they start out . . .
            going out . . seeking the enemy[33]
And they are *afoot*, . .
   they were *afoot* . . on the expedition . . .
And a . . . . the place is . . right near us today,
   our town of Lodge Grass,
      where . . . where this incident . . took place.
They were *afoot*, . .
   coming up the valley . . . (pointing to north)
I would say they're coming up the valley from up the Little Bighorn . .
valley, . .
   from Crow Agency or on up,
      and at the present site of Lodge Grass now, . . .
         they run onto the enemy. (motioning hands together)
The *two men afoot* . . . run onto the enemy
   who are . . . horseback,
      the *Sioux* . . .
They were probably . . a hundred men or so . . .
A *big odd* against the two men . . .
And the time of the day was . . evening,
   nearing . . dark, . .
      darkness is . . falling, . .
         just about to get dark,
   when they were . . *surrounded* . . .
The two men were afoot
   and they were *surrounded* . . by the enemy . . .
A hundred against two or something like that is what we would term. . . .
   the bi-i-g odds against..
So look like a person would think that these two men . . would not have a
chance . . to come [out] alive in that battle . . .

The enemy approached them,
   and they run into them,
      and they found a . . . a *pit*, . . . (motions with hands)
         a dugout . . place,

a washout,
                or something, . .
            near the river . . .
It must be a washout during high water, (motions with hands)
        probably . . we would call it a pit,
                that they found
                        and they *dropped* down into it.
And the enemy was around them,
            shooting at them, (clapping with hands)
                    shooting rifles,
                            arrows at them. . . . (motions with hands)
And they dropped down into that washout, . .
            lay down in there,
                    and arrows would come
                            and stick right by them
                                    that they . . were shot at with arrows . . .
They'd *almost get hit* . . . (gently pats hands together)
They stayed down in there,
            and the enemy surrounded them.
They *could of* . . rushed right on them, . . (claps once with hands)
            and kill them right . . now,
                    but they didn't.
They shoot at them from . . . a little distance,
            probably fifty yards (points off)
                or so,
            around where they were . . hiding in this pit . . .
The enemy, . .
            the Sioux,
                    were all . . . around them,
                            giving them no chance to get away from them at all,
                    they were surrounded,
                            with their weapons shooting at them, (hits fists together)
            and they have no chance,
                    we figure . . .
And . . the enemy shooting at them cross-firing against these . . two men,
            that they were shooting at, (motions with fingers coming together)
                they were all surrounded, . .
            around . . standing close by to each other,
                    so that . . the two men will have no chance to get out,
                            for they are afoot anyway,

and you might think that there's no chance at all for the two men to get
away, . .
      that day, . .
          that evening. . . . .

So . . the headman of the Sioux says,
    "*Wa-a-it a minute now,*
        let's cease fire.
We might accidently shoot . . cross-firing, . . (motions with fingers com-
ing together)
        might hurt each other . . .
So . . let us quit fighting.
These two men have no chance.
We'll *surround them* . . .
Nightfall is coming now, . .
    we'll *surround them,*
        and we'll stay . . in watch tonight . . around them . . .
In the morning when daylight comes, . .
    we'll make a good job of it . . .
We'll approach them . . .
They have no chance.
We'll kill them,
    we'll scalp them,
        and we'll take those honors back with us,
           back home . . .
Those of you . . that count *coups,* (gently pats hands once)
    will do that . . in a good way tomorrow morning.
These two men have no chance.
Let us quit . . firing now,
    for some of us might accidently hurt each other by cross-firing . . .
So stop *shooting.*"
And they stopped. . . .
Those two men there,
    not hit yet, . .
        in that pit . . .
Looking out they were surrounded, (looks around)
    no way of . . getting out. . . .

So . . . Little Head,
    he's the man who had the . . . *medicine,* . . .

The partner maybe a younger man or so,
    not having any medicine, . .
        no way . . for *him* to make medicine to get away
        or anything like that . . .
But . . Little Head . . has the medicine, . .
    he's the medicine man, . .
        he has his medicine *with* him . .
So nightfall came,
    the firing had ceased, . .
        quit firing at them . . .
Nightfall came,
    and they were still there yet, . .
        and they were . . they were surrounded. (points around)

"Now tonight," . .
    the Sioux said,
    "stay close to each other,
        we're all around them,
            these two men.
    They have no chance to get away . . .
    Tomorrow . . when the sun comes up
        and gets bright, . .
            we'll approach them
                we'll kill them, (gently pats hands)
                    we'll . . scalp them
                        we'll . . take their scalps home with us,
                        count coups on them, . . .
                            we'll take back the honors by
                            killing these two men tomor-
                            row morning." . .
So . . . the nightfall came
    and they were all surrounded.
They were there to stand guard around them these two men all night,
    and they would do . . the *killing* the next morning.

So . . after awhile, . .
    after dark, . .
        the young partner of these two men . . says,
            "Little Head,
                why don't you do something?

We must try to get *away* tonight,
    from the enemy, . .
        that is surrounding around us . . .
    Do something!
    You have the medicine,
    I don't have nothing!" . .
Little Head said,
    "That's what I want you to say . . .
    I want you to *ask me* to *make medicine*
        so that we will get away from our enemies that are surrounding . .
        us tonight . . .
    We *will* get away from them!". .
So the young partner said,
    "Now what is he *going to do,* . .
        how are we to *get away* from . . the enemy that is all around
        us?
    We have no chance." . . .
But Little Head said,
    "I wanted you to ask me to do something,
        now I *will* . . . make medicine, . .
            and we'll get away from these . . men around us, .
                so they will not kill us.
    We'll get away from them tonight." . .
"Alright!" . .

So . . Little Head took out his medicine,
    and made . . right in that pit
        with the enemy around him.
He said his prayers, . . (patting hands together)
    whatever he did, . .
        asking his medicine to get them out of there from the enemy, . .
            to escape . . .
So . . the young man . . hoping that . . Little Head's medicine will work . .
    so that they will get away . . alive, . .
        and get away from the enemy, .
            without getting killed . . .

So . . . Little Head made medicine . . . (patting hands together)
When he got *through* he says,

Yellowstone River
near Laurel,
Montana.

"Alright now, . .
　　　we're going to go . .
　　　　　You get behind me.
　　　　　　　Put your arms around my neck,
　　　　　　　　　and . . I'll carry you like a person carrying a
　　　　　　　　　　baby on the back . . (arms held around
　　　　　　　　　　own neck)
　　　　　We're going to *get out* of here . . .
　　　　And . . by *doing* that
　　　　　　I want you to close your eyes (hands over eyes)
　　　　　　　　and never open . . your eyes while we're going
　　　　　　　　　through this . . ceremony.
　　　　Until I tell you to open your eyes,
　　　　　　and you'll open your eyes
　　　　　　　　then we'll be away from here,
　　　　　　　　　　from the enemy,
　　　　　　　　　　　　quite aways . . off.
　　　So . . . mind you that you *close your eyes*, (hands over eyes)
　　　　　and *don't* open your eyes,
　　　　　　　because . . we're going to go!"
The young man said,
　　"Alright!" . . .

He got behind . . Little Head, . .
　　put his arms around him from his back . . . (arms around neck)
He said,
　　"Alright,
　　　　don't open your eyes!" (eyes closed)
When they were getting ready to go,

the young man *opened* his eyes.
Ooo, ooo, ... (disappointment in voice)
    they didn't go! . .
"*I told you you mustn't open your eyes!* (anger in voice)
    Did you?"
And the young man says,
    "Yes." (in a low, quiet voice)
"That's why we didn't go."

"*Now we're going to try it again* . . .
    This time, . .
        remember no-o-t to open your eyes until I . . until I tell you to
        open your eyes! (hands over eyes)
    By that time we will be away from them, . .
        quite aways away,
            for we'll make our *getaway* . . from them . . .
    This time . . if you open your eyes . . *that's* it,
        we're going to get killed,
            we won't go
                and they will kill us tomorrow . . .
    So . . remember,
        don't open your eyes this time!. .
    Now we'll try it again
    Get behind me,
        and put your arms around my me,
            and we're going to *g-o-o!*" (claps hands and then drops
        arms to floor)
So . . the young man said,
    "Alright!
        I'll try and not open my eyes this time."

Put his arms around him . . .
He said,
    "*Okay,*
        we're going!" . .
(hard clap with hands)
They flew away like *birds*,
    flying away from their perch,
        tree,
            or something!

They went up in the air . . up in the air,
    and . . on over the enemy,
        and in the dark the enemy didn't see them . . .
They *flew up out of there* into the air, . .
    and *sailed . . a mile away* (hands raised to sky)
        or so, . .
            where they land . .
There the enemy were there,
    on the ground,
        they didn't know they were gone . . .
They flew away like *birds*, .
    flying away . . .
They *went out* of there,
    landed . . a mile away
        or so,
            in the dark . . .

When they landed . . . Little Head said,
    "*Alright,*
        open your eyes!"
And the young man opened his eyes
    and they were . . away . . *away* from that place,
        somewhere else they landed.
"*Now we'll go!*
    we're *afoot*,
        we'll *travel* tonight." . .
They probably went north . . down the Little Bighorn . . . (points south)
By daylight,
    they were *wa-a-y down* by Crow Agency
        or somewhere, . .
            far away from the enemy . .

Daylight come,
    Sun come up bright . . .
The Sioux said,
    "*Alright,*
        let's approach now.
        We'll get them!" . .
They approached down to the pit,
    looking in there,

and they were gone,
　　　　　they were not there.
So they didn't get to kill these two men,
　　　　they got away . . .
These two men were alive,
　　　　they got away, . .
　　　　　　　and went on home . .
So the enemy didn't get them . . .
So . . . that's the great *medicine* that Little Head had,
　　　　that . . made them get away from the enemy
　　　　　　　without . . getting killed . . .
They missed . . killing those two,
　　　　and they couldn't do . . anything.
"They're *gone*!
　　　　We don't know what way, . .
　　　　　　　they got away from us . . somewhere . . .
　　　　Surely they didn't get in,
　　　　　　　for we were close around them,
　　　　　　　　　　close together that they can't get in between us.
　　　　We were on the *watch* for them.
　　　　They got away someway."
They didn't know! . .

But that's . . *great medicine* of Little Head, . . .
　　　　work real good, . . .
　　　　　　　that saved their lives
　　　　　　　　　and they got home, . . .
　　　　　　　　　　　back to their people . . .

I

The Texture

"Feel It"

As you may have sensed as you "entered" the previous stories, the particular qualities the storyteller brings to the telling significantly influences both the accessibility and meaning of that story. This may have been most noticeable in the stories of Lawrence Aripa, Tom Yellowtail, and Mari Watters. Our concern in this chapter is not so much with what is being conveyed in the oral literature—the cultural themes and literary motifs—but how those themes and motifs are presented and engaged. We will review several of the qualities that distinguish orality from literacy, introduce some of the key techniques of storytelling used by raconteurs, and discuss the particular capacity of the spoken word to affect the world. When you enter the story, you have to "feel it."

Orality and Literacy

As we come to an appreciation of an oral literature, we need to clarify many of the salient qualities that contrast orality and literacy.[1] The oral literature of the Inland Peoples emanates from a tradition in which the prominent mode of communication is in speech. It is a tradition akin to that in which Homer in the eighth century B.C. produced the *Iliad* and the *Odyssey*. It is the tradition that lives in over 3,000 other viable oral-based languages spoken throughout the world today. Of all the languages spoken, less than eighty are grounded in their own derived literacy.

It must be pointed out that orality is not synonymous

with *illiteracy*, which refers to the lack of literacy skills within a literacy-based tradition and not to the presence of orality skills in such a tradition. In addition, the speech patterns found in literacy-based cultures, such as our own, are significantly grounded in literacy structures and forms and are not equivalent per se to the speech patterns found in oral-based cultures. These two important observations became most apparent to me after I had lived for several years in a community in which Apsáalooke was the primary language and then acquired sufficient competency in Apsáalooke to converse with Crows and to satisfy my foreign language requirement in graduate school (though I am still far from fluent).

In distinguishing orality from literacy, however, we should not go so far as to see one form of expression as exclusive of the other. The particular language configuration of any given culture can, in fact, exemplify qualities of both orality and literacy. Indeed, the pictorial arts of oral-based cultures—as represented in pictographs, ritual costumes and masks, sacred fetishes and objects, and architectural structures and adornments—can embrace many of the qualities I will suggest as indicative of literacy. In turn, the significance of orality in a literacy-based culture cannot be underestimated. Any given culture must be assessed as to its own unique linguistic configuration. It is much more appropriate to approach orality and literacy in terms of a continuum. The following comments are meant to stimulate your thinking and should not be construed as being the definitive word on the subject.

Let us first look at what is most elemental and basic: the physiological experience of orality and literacy. Orality is fundamentally an auditory experience composed of morphemes, that is, meaningful clusters of sound. There is a flow of sound, but no visual presence. As a physiological phenomenon, orality is an evanescent and transitory event, existing only when it is going out of existence. Further, orality is an experience in which the sound envelops and surrounds the listener. It can unify the listener with the source of the sound. Once it is emitted, the sound is heard. The ears are not easily "closed." Orality is thus a transitory *event* that *unifies* the listener *involuntarily* with the sound and its source.

To the extent that the character of the medium (the experience of speech as an event) influences that to which it refers (the images of the world), orality tends to reveal a world in terms of *action*, *process* and *becoming*. As we have already seen, transformation is an underlying theme within the stories. It may be expressed in a creation account as Coyote frees the Salmon, gives Rattlesnake his particular character, or creates the various peoples from the parts of the Monster. In "Burnt Face" and "Seal Boy," each protagonist is transformed—one boy's face is made "as good as when he was first born" and another boy is made to be at "home down in the water" among the Seals. The world is revealed and conceptualized as an *event*.[2]

In contrast, the physiological experience of literacy is composed of visual images, that is, of written words affixed to a page. Literacy is as an object, with a more-or-less permanent presence. It has a "thingness" quality. Writing is, after all, housed in the ink that appears on the paper found in a book. The viewer can voluntarily select that which he or she chooses to view or can ignore it altogether; the viewer can close his or her eyes. In this sense, literacy is directional and focused, allowing the viewer to select and dissect from the field of visual experience. It isolates and creates "words." There are no isolated words, per se, in orality. In fact, it may be difficult to identify a term for word in an American Indian language. Thus literacy as a physiological experience has a *permanence*; it is an *object* that allows the viewer to *voluntarily* select and focus on isolated words.

To the extent that the character of the medium (the experience of literacy as an object) influences that to which it refers (the images of the world), the world tends to be revealed as an object, in terms of concreteness and permanence. The world is conceptualized as an object, *objectified*.

It should be noted, however, that these physiological qualities should not be equated with the residual and retentive aspects of orality and literacy. Despite the transitory character of sound, peoples in oral-based cultures have a tremendous capacity to remember, in detail, elaborate and lengthy oral narratives, passing them down virtually unchanged, generation after generation. In addition, while the spoken word possess an evanescent quality, it can certainly elicit vivid and lasting images in the mind of the listener. And by contrast, as any librarian or teacher will attest, to affix words to permanent objects, for example, books, does not ensure their continued usage, nor even their very existence.

The capacity to "remember a story" was impressively demonstrated to me several years ago while I was teaching on the Crow Reservation. I was the instructor for a group of graduate students home for the summer, enrolled in an off-campus course in Native American Religion. A "honky" teaching Indians about Indian religion is a story unto itself! But the students were kind to me, we shared much, and all were eager to explore traditions not so familiar. While each student was well accomplished in literacy and fluent in English, all were nevertheless grounded in the oral tradition. Each spoke Apsáalooke as his or her primary language. Priding myself in the materials I had prepared for the course, I soon became concerned and then annoyed when none of my students took diligent notes on my lectures. I would have my day— the midterm exam would be based extensively on my lectures! But the day, it turned out, belonged to my students. They had "remembered" in detail that which I had spoken in lecture form, and, in turn, they conveyed it with elegance in their blue books! They did not need to rely upon the written word, on note taking, to retain what was an elaborate and relatively large body of new knowledge.

The ways in which meaning and knowledge are elicited, organized, stored, and communicated in the two traditions significantly differ. In orality, meaning is inexorably interwoven in the immediacy of human experience; it is *contextualized*. Meaningful morphemes emanate out of an integrated social context involving interpersonal dynamics, gesturing and intonation by the speaker, and listener responses, as well as a shared syntax and semantics. There can be no meaning without its being spoken within a social context. Among the Crow, there are subtle variances in the intonation patterns in certain words, all dependent upon the age and gender of the speaker. The meaning of a particular word can be significantly altered, depending on the intonation voiced by an older woman or by a younger man. Personal pronouns (he, she, it) are not distinguished in the Crow language. Only in the larger context of usage can gender distinctions be determined in speech. As you may have noticed, Crow storytelling minimizes the use of function words such as prepositions (about, for, of, with) and conjunctions (and, but, or, both). In fact, the character of the language found in all our story texts is rather terse. Separate morphemes, and the meaningful ideas they represent, are tied together by the particular gesturing and intonation used by the storyteller, not necessarily by the actual words uttered. A teller may glance in a certain direction and point a finger, and all eyes will look off, but there are no words spoken. The meaning embedded in the narratives is not reducible to the words alone; it is rendered out of an entire context of social interactions.

Similarly, knowledge itself is organized, stored, and communicated in *narrative-based structures of human experiential action*. Knowledge is embedded within stories and their telling, in ritual dance and song, in various art and architectural forms, in dress and costumes, and throughout the landscape as a mythic geography. The rock outcropping and riverbeds, the fall of snow and the coming of the salmon tell a story, like a text conveying knowledge. The stories are repeated each winter, told aloud by the elders. Most importantly, all these stories are experienced directly and personally. The song is sung, the dress worn, the lodge lived in, the path along the river traveled, the story felt. Each time the rocks are heated and the sweat lodge entered, the story and its meaning are reiterated. You directly participate in this knowledge. "When the story ended, . . . you look and see, see the story; we are linked."

In literacy, meaning is independent of the immediate human context and texture, having a *formalized* and *autonomous* syntax and semantics. A written sentence can have meaning without the gestures of a speaker or the responses of listeners. For instance, the inclusion of conjunctions allows linkage of separate words. A sentence can stand on its own. Meaning is rendered much more decontextualized.

In turn, knowledge is organized, stored, and communicated in an elaborate set of *standardized, formalized, and abstract categories and literary forms.* Knowledge is embedded within histories, biographies, and various literary and technical genres and within lists, indexes, tables, data, calendars, textbooks, dictionaries, essays, novels, and archival records. "History" is made possible. In fact, all these media and expressions come into their very existence through literacy. Words can be isolated and given comprehensive and definitive meanings. There are "correct" ways of writing and using words, a proper grammar. Words, and the knowledge conveyed by them, are not sung, worn, danced, or traveled. Knowledge is thus much more formalized, abstracted from direct experience.

With literacy there is also the possibility of "backward scanning," of analysis of the lined texts. Words can be scrutinized and dissected. Symbolic logic and calculus, and the assumptions and methodology of the scientific method—that is, empiricism and rationalism—are facilitated. However, this is not to suggest that peoples in oral-based traditions lack the mental abilities to think abstractly, rationally, or empirically.

Literacy does not determine modes of thinking, but rather channels and provides alternative and additional parameters for revealing, processing, storing, and communicating knowledge.

In conclusion (and with reference to some of the implications for the oral literature of Inland Peoples), orality tends to direct attention toward action, process, and *becoming* (the world viewed is expressed through an event—speech), toward *involvement* (the experience of orality is involuntary), toward *social interaction* and *integration* (requiring a social context to elicit meaning), and toward renewal and *return* (as expressed in the cyclic organization of time and space). In orality, meaning and knowledge are *contextualized* within a network of interpersonal and experiential relations. Orality is necessarily a *social* event, involving at least a speaker and a listener. Orality tends to be *participatory.*

In contrast, literacy tends to direct attention toward the *appearance* of *objects* (the world viewed is expressed through ink on paper in books—objects), toward *selection* and the possibility of *disengagement* (the experience of literacy is voluntary), toward *linearity* (as expressed in spatial and temporal organization), and toward *history* (reliance on archival records based in linear time—years, decades, centuries, millennia). In literacy, meaning and knowledge are *formalized* into autonomous, self-contained words. In contrast with orality, words are *decontextualized*, seldom "worn"; they are estranged from direct human experience. Participation is not needed to complete the meaning of a word. Literacy is fundamentally a solitary experience; both the writer and the reader communicate in privacy, alone from each other. Literacy can *objectify* and *distance* the events of the world from the experiences of the individual.

Techniques of Storytelling

The orality of the literature is further characterized by the particular techniques of storytelling[3]. The Coeur d'Alene term for storytelling is *me-y-mi-ym,* meaning "he/she is going to tell stories." In the various techniques, the storyteller endeavors to transform the listeners of the story into participants within the story. During the telling of a Coyote story, for instance, it is difficult to be an onlooker, passive and nonengaged. In fact, participation within the story must be overtly acknowledged throughout the telling, if the telling is to continue. During the telling of a story, Coyote or otherwise, individuals periodically respond by saying, ée (in Apsáalooke) or *i··!* (in Salish), meaning "yes." Among the Pend d'Oreille, participation is acknowledged by making the hand sign for "I got it," hooking the index finger and drawing it in toward the body. As long as the responses are given, the telling continues. But should they cease, so too would the story. There is no one in the story any longer!

Everyone has the potential to be a storyteller. Indeed, modes of storytelling pervade even everyday language and conversation. Sitting down for an evening meal can mean much more than the consumption of good food, as the stories continue into the late-evening hours. When trying to describe the behavior of someone else, a person may almost instinctively slip in an abbreviated account of Old Man Coyote, using the example of Coyote to convey the point. It is as if the behavior of the individual in question is modeled after the example set by Coyote. According to Mari Watters, a Nez Perce storyteller, "everyone tells stories, everyone is a storyteller."

Nevertheless, certain qualities greatly enhance a storyteller's ability to bring a narrative to "life" and transform the listeners into participants. The language of the storyteller is often colored with a *dramatic* use of *intonation, pauses,* even the *speech mannerisms* of the animal people. Grizzly Bear's warning is heard in a voiced growl. "Bear comes up, Gra-ah, r-a-a-ah!" Silence can be as meaningful as the spoken word. Pauses are used to highlight and add drama. "I'll catch up to you, . . . and . . . chew out your windpipe!" Words are often spoken slowly, with deliberation. The volume of the voice may rise and fall, the pitch may change, accenting this action or that character in the story. "And Coyote *stood* up, and said *'It's me, Coyote!'*" in a clear, loud voice. Augmenting the voice is the language of *hand* and *body gestures*—visual images. The storyteller may look off to the distance with surprise in his eyes and say, "And so . . . *Coyote* is going along," and the listeners look off as well! Each instance when Tom Yellowtail makes reference to "here" and "there" within his stories, a hand, an arm, or perhaps a finger will motion in some direction. As some of the elders speak a story into being, they also motion in traditional sign language.

While the length of the narratives can be extensive, the actual language used in the stories is generally rather *terse*. Coyote's actions are stated simply. "It's Old Man Coyote. He is going around, very hungry." And not only are Coyote's actions understated, his emotions and motivations as well as his very physical being are seldom described in detail. They are only hinted at. As Archie Phinney said, "No clear image is offered or needed." Similarly, while the mythic geography is specified—each of the rivers named, for instance—seldom is it painted with the color of flowers, the texture of trees, or the song of birds. "Coyote . . . was going upstream. *Coyote* is a-always going upstream. And . . he's going upstream, and he's going along the Clearwater . . ." As a consequence, by only loosely defining the image, action, and disposition of narrative characters and scenes, the terse language of the story invites each listener to contribute his or her own particular images to the story. The story's landscape and characters are given added color and textural detail through the active imaginations of those participating within that story.

The stories are *linked to the seasons* as well as to daily events. Typically, the long winter evenings are the season for storytelling. In the Plateau area, storytelling often corresponds to the sacred Winter Dances.

Among the Crow, stories of Old Man Coyote should not be told during the summer—"bad things just happen!" His season is from the first frost in the fall until the first thunder is heard the following spring. This is the season when "the snakes and the bears are asleep and won't pay you a visit; they really like joining in!" As you feel the cold winter's wind, you know the voice of Coyote is not far away. Similarly, when the tipis are being set up at Crow Fair each August or the first winter's sweat bath is taken, there is always a particular story told. As you drive down the highway, that coulee, this bend in the river, or that rock outcropping is pointed to and its story told. As you undergo a season, visit a locale, or experience an event, you participate in its story.[4]

Coyote's stories are often interwoven into a single narrative cycle that accounts for his entire journey up the Columbia and its various tributaries, culminating in the "coming of the people." Such a cycle cannot be completed in a single sitting, however. Clarence Woodcock, a Pend d'Oreille, remembers how it would take his father three consecutive winter nights, from sunset to sunrise, to tell the story of Coyote. And no one would think of deleting this section or shortening that segment of the cycle. The point of the telling is as much to participate in the grand adventures as it is to enjoy the character of Coyote.

The length of the narrative is also the consequence of stylistic phrase and sequence *repetition*. The storyteller can choose to emphasize a particular action by repeating key phrases or ideas. Perhaps to highlight the challenge as well as the distance to be traveled in Plenty Hawk's account of Burnt Face's quest, the young man is seen setting up four camps and being carried on the backs of four groups of Ducks, each of a different color. The number of repetitions in a story often depends on the dominant number pattern of that tradition. Among the Crow, as with many other Plains-area peoples, this number pattern is likely four. Old Man Coyote should not use the bell "four times." Burnt

Mari Watters, 1991.

Face heats four sweat stones and waits through four fogs in confrontation with the Long Otter. Throughout most of the Plateau area, three and five are the dominant numbers. It takes Fox three jumps over Coyote to revive him from the "dead." Coyote and Swallowing Monster try to "draw each other in" three times and Coyote makes five flint knives to cut the heart. Coyote is told by his younger Sisters to sweat for five days, using five bunches of rocks. It takes Coyote five digging sticks and five attempts to break the Swallow Sisters' dam. It is then in the last attempt—be it the third, the fourth, or the fifth—that the myth person succeeds or is foiled.

As Dell Hymes has pointed out, patterned numbers also shape the groupings of verses within traditional spoken narratives.[5] A storyteller indicates individual verses (as indicated by separate lines in the narrative texts here) through the use of intonation, extended pauses, or quotative suffixes ("he said"). The clusterings of verses is organized according to the dominant number pattern of the tradition. Among the Nez Perce, Klamath, and Klikitat, for instance, three- and five-verse groupings are typically found. Each set of verse groupings, in turn, may represent a scene. Scenes designate groupings of action related to a given locale and characters in the story and are suggested by the narrative's plot and its line groupings. The entire structure of the narrative text is organized in this way.

Fifty years ago, Tom Yellowtail, along with his wife, Susie, and several other Crows, toured the capitals of Europe for six months as a traditional dance troupe. Leaving rural Montana, visiting the historic sites of Europe, and performing before royalty and dignitaries in itself offered quite a story; and upon their return, the family gathered around to hear Tom tell it. As a seasoned raconteur, Tom told the story with all the techniques and nuances, with all the repetitions appropriate for the telling. An hour went by, midnight passed and by the early morning hours, all were silent. No one could stay in the story any longer. Yet by then, Tom had only told of going from Wyola, Montana, to New York City! He hadn't even gotten on the boat to Europe.

While the various storytelling techniques just outlined might be used by any raconteur, they are not necessarily to be found equally in all storytellers. There is, in fact, a tremendous range in the storytelling styles used by individual storytellers. This is particularly evident in the stories of Lawrence Aripa and Tom Yellowtail. Tom relies extensively on hand gestures and phrase repetition, and he always anchors his stories in a geographic location. In contrast, Lawrence adds drama to his stories by more frequent placement of emphasis on certain key morphemes, as reflected in his use of intonation and extension of vowel sounds. "*A-a-ah, I slept* a lo-o-ng time!"

But there is one ability I find associated with *all* storytellers—the ability to remember. Mari Watters once demonstrated an amazing capacity for remembering a story just told her. We were seated around a campfire, and one among us had just completed his telling of a Lakota story. He was an accomplished teller himself and told the narrative with detail and twists, speaking for some twenty minutes. At the end of that story, Mari said, "Let's see if I got it," and immediately retold the entire story. But it was not a rote memorization that we heard. She added her imprint and told it with her own "heart."

In the context of storytelling, stories are always re-membered, never memorized. Memorization results in a rigidity that can inhibit participation in the story. Remembering encourages spontaneity and thus greater immediacy with the listener. Remembering has an important additional significance. To remember is to return to, to reunite with the reality within the story, to reestablish membership with the characters of the story. The storyteller seeks that membership for the listeners as well as for himself or herself.

It is instructive to note here that the Crow term for storytelling, *baaeechichiwaau,* literally means "retelling one's own." Traditionally, to tell a story was to own that story. The right to tell a story was obtained either through direct purchase of the story or as the result of having received the story as a gift from another. We saw the importance of "retelling one's own" in "Four Smokes" and "Burnt Face" (Yellowtail version). In both cases, upon being reunited with the entire camp, the young men tell of their experiences. The story told has become part of the teller, an extension of his or her very being. Storytelling involves the retelling—the "re-membering," if you will—of one's own story.

It is perhaps this quality of re-membering that above all else distinguishes an oral literature. If a story is to come to life, it must be energized with the participation of the listeners as well as the teller, all dancing alongside the characters of the story. Whenever I heard Lawrence Aripa or Tom Yellowtail tell his stories in the company of a host of others, the stories always had a certain spark and dynamic. I saw, reflected in the eyes of those participating, the image of Coyote. But when those same stories were shared with me, alone, without membership, they seemed flat by comparison.

This special quality of re-membering first became apparent to me several years ago while I was living with the Yellowtail family at their home in Wyola. Tom and Susie were as generous as they were gifted storytellers. The fact is, Susie was as skilled in storytelling as was Tom, and she had an important story to tell. She was the first American Indian to become a registered nurse in this country. She received her nurse's education "back East," in Boston, where she had to change her name, since "Susie Walking Bear frightened the patients!" Married to an *akbaalía,* "one who doctors," and a man who "ran" Sun Dances, Susie was herself very active in traditional healing and religious practices. She traveled with Tom to Europe; and the "sights they saw!" Susie served on presidential commissions; she chaperoned "Miss American Indian" winners as they toured the country; and she was in constant demand on college campuses as a speaker. Susie indeed had a story to tell!

And tell it she did. Each weekend, especially during the summer months, Susie would be visited by "friends and strangers" seeking to hear her story. And each weekend I might be on hand to listen as well. Though most interesting to be sure, after a few sittings, I grew restless and sometimes turned away. And then I noticed something in the course of those weekends. Tom, her husband of fifty-plus years, sat there each weekend, listening to the stories; the man who had probably shared in the experiences from which the stories sprang did not turn away. In fact, he would laugh, and cry, and act as if he had never heard the story before! Susie told her stories with such skill that Tom was remembered within them. The stories were alive. And then I too began participating.

Power in Words

The summer I interviewed Alan Old Horn, I was participating in an ethnographic project designed to improve understanding and relations between the Indian Health Service physicians and their Crow patients. Tensions had been growing for some time, in part because the physicians had little awareness of their patients' cultural values relating to health and healing. I was to gather information on the Crow perspective of

Susie Yellowtail, 1977.

health and healing and prepare a background paper for the physicians. While everyone I worked with was excited about the project and was most cooperative, there was one problem. For many of the most traditional families, when it got down to discussing the actual afflictions of a member of the family, few would talk about them. And then I was introduced to the Crow word, *dasshússua,* literally meaning, "breaking with the mouth." That which comes through the mouth, words, has the power to affect the world. People were reluctant to discuss an illness for fear of bringing forth that affliction.

I soon began to appreciate *dasshússua* in other ways.

For instance, one does not say "goodbye" upon departing after a good evening's visit, but rather "I'll see you later," *diiawákaawik*. "Goodbye is too final, you may not see them again!" And one should always do exactly what he or she has publicly stated would be done; otherwise, "accidents seem to happen." When you need to convey something publicly before the tribal council, at a giveaway, or during a ceremony such as a Sun Dance, it is best to convey it through an "announcer," someone older, more experienced in the use of words, someone who would not inadvertently abuse them, someone like Alan Old Horn. An announcer may even have a medicine bundle for the proper use of words.

When it is time for a child to receive an "Indian name," a clan uncle or aunt is consulted. Having "dreamt" the name, the namer then bestows it upon the child in a ceremony involving an opened medicine bundle and prayer. At that time you might hear a voiced concern—"I hope the name agrees with the child!" If the words of the name agree with the disposition of the child, the child grows to become the words of his or her name. But should the name disagree, the child will become sickly and a new name must be sought. The "Indian name" is not one's public name, but to be used in prayer and at sacred ceremonies. It is the name that guides and protects one. More than one war veteran has come back "unscratched," protected because of his or her "Indian name."

Without doubt, the spoken word has a power, *baax-pée,* a creative force to affect the world. In the context of storytelling, this has particular significance. As the fibers of the words are woven into the exquisite tapestry of a story, the words bring forth the deeds portrayed. The animation of a story literally occurs in voicing the words of that story. The words of the narrative do not just describe the events referred to in the story, they help bring them about. The stories are to be

A story in the garden, Tom Yellowtail, June 1993.

entered with great respect and responsibility. They should never be taken lightly. For the *words* of the stories *make the world*.

This understanding is consistently expressed in the oral literature. In the Sanpoil story, "Sweat Lodge," that follows, naming the various animals and birds is an integral part of creating and bringing forth those beings. In a Nez Perce story, when Coyote says he wants to look like his son and then like a Flathead man shooting grouse, Coyote becomes his son and then becomes the Flathead man. In the Wasco story of Coyote freeing the fish, Coyote says to the two Sisters that they will become swallows, and so they do. When Coyote speaks the words, "Shush ta-ways-s ta-lee-e," the logs he is on go apart. In a Kootenai narrative, when a man named "Wolf" says and sings his name, he becomes a wolf. As reflected in the Kootenai story, "Star Husband," when a girl says, "That is a nice little star there. I'll marry him," she finds herself married. When a story comes to an end or an entire cycle is completed for the season, Clackamas storytellers tell the myth people spoken of in the narratives to go to the mountains, to the rivers, into the air, into the animals of the forests, the fishes of the waters, and the birds of the sky.[6] That which had been spoken and

witnessed in the storytelling was indeed alive and now
free to return to a world mythically endowed.

|

SWEAT LODGE

JIM JAMES, SANPOIL[7]

Sweat Lodge was chief long,
    long ago.
But he wasn't called Sweat Lodge then.
He was just called chief.

He decided to create all the animals and all the birds.
So he created them
    and *named* them all.
He *named* each animal and each bird.

Then he *told* each one of them,
    "In times to come,
        when people have been created,
            and they send their children out,
                during the day or during the night,
        you *talk* with them,
        and *tell* them what they will be able to do when they grow up.
You will *tell* the boys that they are to get things easily,
    are to be good hunters,
        good fishermen,
            good gamblers,
                and so on.
You will *tell* the girls that they will be able to get things easily.
All that time I will be Sweat Lodge, myself."

Then he *spoke* to them again,
    "I'll have no body,
        no head,
            nor will I be able to see.
Whoever desires to construct me will have the right to do so.
The one that builds me may pray to me for good looks,
    or whatever he may wish,
        the one that made me.

Crow sweat lodge.

I'll take pity on him,
    and I'll give him what he requests,
        the one that made me.
Thus people may approach me,
    if anyone is injured,
        or if he is sick,
            or if he is poisoned,
                he may come to me for help,
                    and I'll give it to him.
    Also, when anyone is dying,
        he may come to me,
            and I'll help him then also.

I'll help him see the next world.
So in this world I am Sweat Lodge,
for the help of human beings."

|

STAR HUSBAND
BARNABY, KOOTENAI[8]

Well, I'll tell a story of how a girl was married to a star.

The people of olden times live in a tent.
Two girls went out.

When they were about to go to sleep,
    one of them looked up.
She saw many stars.
She saw a small one,
    and said,
        "That is a nice little star there.
           I'll marry him."
Then the two girls laughed when she said so.
They went in again.

After they had slept,
    early in the morning she woke up.
There was talking,
    and she knew that those were not voices of her parents.
She arose,
    and she saw that she did not know the people.
She was sitting down next to an old man.
She knew that she was married to him.

She saw many other young men.
She thought,
    "When there are many youths,
        why don't they marry me?"
    My husband is old."
He said to her,
    "Here I am!
    The other night you said to me,

'You little nice one!
            Marry me.'
      Now I have taken you."
She looked at the large stars.
Now, these were the young men.
The little stars were the old ones.
Then the girl cried when she saw that she had been taken from her country.
She stayed there.

The Star Women were digging roots.
The girl went along with them.
She was told,
      "Don't break the ground where there is a tree."
The girl thought,
      "What do the stars mean?"

There was a tree,
      and she dug up the ground.
The ground was just thin.
She thought she would look,
      and down below she saw this world.
She recognized her relatives walking about.
Then she cried.
She made something,
      and tied herself to it,
            and let herself down.

Then she met her relatives.
They said,
      "Where did you go?
            We lost you."
She said,
      "When I said I would marry the little star,
            then after I had slept,
                  when I woke up,
                        I saw a Star coming down for me.
      I married the Star.
      The little one was an old man.
      The large stars were young people."
Then she told what she had done and how she had come down.

The Star noticed that she was not coming back.
He looked for her.
She had gone down again.

At night they slept.
The next morning when they got up,
    it was noticed that the girl would not rise.
They looked at her for a long time.
Then it became known that she was dead.
She was killed by the Star whom she had left.
He struck her down.

Now I have told you what a girl did.

|

COYOTE AND THE GREEN SPOT
LAWRENCE ARIPA, COEUR D'ALENE[9]

One day Coyote was feeling good.
He was running along the . . St. Joe River,
    having a good time,
        just *romping*
           just *jumping*
              and . . trying to have fun.
But he was all alone.
Nobody else there to . . join him.
So he just goes
    and he has *a lot* of fun.
He runs up the banks
    down the banks
        through the brushes,
           singing
              and hollering. (rapid voice)

And all of a sudden he stops, ...
    and he looks, . . .
        and it was a very . . warm . . spring day.
And he looks *way up* across the river,
    and *way up* . . on the hill . . there is a *real* . . *green* . . spot,
        just beautiful

the Sun hit it
　　　　and it just shone
　　and it was *just* beautiful.
He stops
　　and he looks,
　　　　and he says,
　　　　　　"Wo-o-w, . . I'll bet you there are a lot of *mice*,
　　　　　　　　I'll bet you I could have a lot of fun.
　　　　　　That's beautiful."
And he says,
　　"I am going . . to go up there."

And he starts
　　and gets to the river.
And he sees the water.
And he says,
　　"O-o-h, I don't know how to *swim!*"
He says,
　　"I can't go across.
　　　　I'll have to find some way to make it." . .
So he turns
　　and he starts walking along the bank . . trying to figure a way to get
　　across.

And then he runs across . . Mrs. Mole.
And Mrs. Mole says,
　　"*Ahh, haa,* Coyote, . . again you are planning something mischievous.
　　What are you trying to do?"
So he told . . Mrs. Mole.
He said,
　　"You see that place up there, . .
　　　　it's all beautiful?
　　I want to go there.
　　But I can't get across the river,
　　　　because I never learned to swim."
Mrs. Mole says,
　　"Well, if you go *down* about five or six miles there is a shallow place,
　　　　and you can walk across."
And the Coyote says,
　　"No that's *too far.*

No, I'll find another way."
And Mrs. Mole says,
 "*Coyote,* you are going to do something wrong again.
  When you get that look on your face,
   you *always* do something." (light laughter from audience)
And she says,
 "I'm *warning* you!
  Watch yourself.
   Don't do it!"
And he says,
 "Well, I don't know what I'm going to do,
  but I'm going to get across the river."

So . . she leaves him
 and then he goes on his way.
"What can I do?
 How can I get across?"
And he's . . a wandering
 going back and forth.
And all of a sudden there is a voice . . *way* far off, . . (voice fades off)
 "Shush ta-ways-s ta-lee-e, chacha ta-ways-s ta-lee-e.
 Shush ta-ways-s ta-lee-e, chacha ta-ways-s ta-lee-e."
And he thought,
 "That's a human voice!
  I wonder what that *is*?"

So he . . goes up to the river,
 and then he goes along the bank
  and he gets in the brush,
   and he pushes the brush aside.
He looks on the river
 and there in the middle of the river . . is a little boy . .
  standing on two logs . . .
And then he says,
 "Shush ta-ways-s ta-lee-e,"
  and the logs go apart.
And then he says,
 "Chacha ta-ways-s ta-lee-e,"
  and they come back again.
"Shush ta-ways-s ta-lee-e, chacha ta-ways-s ta-lee-e.

Shush ta-ways-s ta-lee-e, chacha ta-ways-s ta-lee-e."
And he kept on a going
        and he is moving . .
And the Coyote says,
        "A-a-h, . . *that's how* I'll get across! (laughter from audience)
                I'll have to get . . those logs.
                    Those logs have special powers!"

So he goes back into the brush
        and he starts hollering, . .
            "*Help, help,*
                I'm being *murdered*!
                    Help, *help me*!" (in a weak, distant voice followed by
                    laughter from audience)
And so he ye-e-lls. (laughter continues)
And so the little boy hears it.
And so he turns the logs
        and says,
            "Shush ta-ways-s ta-lee-e, chacha ta-ways-s ta-lee-e."
And he go-o-es to the bank.
He jumps off
        and he . . tries to figure out where the noise come from.
And so he runs
        and he gets up on the bank
            and he's *looking* around,
                and he don't see anything.

In the meantime the Coyote *run* down to the logs
        he *jumped* on
                and he looked down. (all in a very rapid voice)
                    "Let's see now,
                        what was that?" (in a quiet, questioning voice)
He looked down
        and he says,
            "Shush ta-ways-s ta-lee-e,"
                and they started to go apart.
"Shush ta-ways-s ta-lee-e, chacha ta-ways-s ta-lee-e.
        Shush ta-ways-s ta-lee-e."
And he start *moving* out . . onto the river.
And boy he was *happy*.

And the little boy come running back to the bank
and he . . started hollering.
But the Coyote was already way out there.

And that was *wonderful,*
"Shush ta-ways-s ta-lee-e, chacha ta-ways-s ta-lee-e.
Shush ta-ways-s ta-lee-e, chacha ta-ways-s ta-lee-e."
"*Why,* . . that's *good.*"
And he started getting more and more excited. (rapid, excited voice)
And all of a sudden he start going fast,
"Shush ta-ways-s ta-lee-e, chacha ta-ways-s ta-lee-e.
Shush ta-ways-s ta-lee-e, chacha ta-ways-s ta-lee-e." (very rapid voice)
And the logs were going . . back and forth
and he was *moving* . . . (laughter by audience)

And then he looked
and turned back to see where the boy was,
and then . . . something . . snapped.
And he says,
"Shush ta-ways-s ta-lee-e."
And they start to go.
And he kept looking around. (laughter continues)
He couldn't think . . . how to get them back.
He couldn't think . . of those words.
And so the logs keep coming apart, (rapid voice, laughter continues)
"Shush ta-ways-s ta-lee-e.
Shush ta-ways-s ta-lee-e.
Shush ta-ways-s ta-lee-e." (rapid voice, a lot of laughter)
And the logs keep going
and the Coyote fell in, . .
and he *drowned* . . . (tremendous laughter by audience)

So . . his body floated . . down the river,
and . . then he gets hooked on a . . *branch* . . in the river.
And here comes Mrs. Mole,
"I haven't heard from that silly thing for a long time.
He must be in trouble!" (laughter from audience)
So she runs up and down . . the river
and all of a sudden she looks into the river
and there . . he's hooked up on that . . branch.

So she goes
>   and she gets him
>>   and she pulls him out.

And she says,
>   "That silly, silly bad Coyote.
>>   He's done it again!"

So she calls on her special powers.
And then she *jumps* over him,
>   three times.

And then . . all of a sudden . . he opens his eyes
>   and,
>>   "*A-a-a-h, I slept* a lo-o-ng time!" (big yawning voice)

And she says,
>   "*Slept*?
>>   You were *dead*!" (laughter)

And she says,
>   "It's all because . . you are *foolish*! . .
>>   You have to *lea-r-rn* . . to be better.
>>>   You have to *list-en* to what people tell you. . . .
>   Things aren't always *greener* on the other side!" (laughter from
>   audience)

And also . . she told him . . that,
>   "It's your fault because you *tried* something you're *not* used to,
>>   it's something you don't know anything about.
>   You didn't know the language,
>>   and you got mixed up.
>   And that's how you *drowned*!" . . .

I

The Context

"You've Gotta Go Inside"

*W*hy are the stories told? And to whom are they told? Two pivotal questions, the responses to which place the oral literature of the Inland Peoples in its proper context.

A Time for Stories

The fire was just beginning to die down, revealing a bed of red-hot coals and rock. Tessa, a great-granddaughter, was splashing about in the cool spring water of the creek that ran just in front of us. As we sat on folding chairs and waited for our sweat bath, Tom Yellowtail pointed to the hillside and the charred brush and told of "the fire that got away."

> And TR [one of Tom's sons] was alone out here, about to take a sweat, when the fire spread fast. The grass was pretty dry around here and a lot of acres caught fire. And the cowboys from over the ridge saw the smoke and came to see what was going on. And there was TR, in shorts, sunglasses, wearing a beret, trying to put the fire out with a blanket! [a big laugh from Tom] A lot of acres burned, but the grass came up better than ever this spring!

Even as we walked back from the sweat to the cabin, there was a story. And the stories continued into the late-evening hours.

For some time now, David, Tom's grandson, had wanted to hear the story of Burnt Face. After the sweat, a wonderful buffalo roast "with all the trimmings" was served for dinner. With Tom at the head, and David and me on either side of the cleared table,

169

and with great-grandchildren comfortably seated on the sofa, Tom finally began the story of Burnt Face. The words came out cautiously at first, slow but deliberate. As the story unfolded, the words, still chosen with deliberation, flowed with great ease. Hands that had at first been still in Tom's lap now rose and fell frequently, giving visual imagery to the spoken words. An arm would be raised and a finger pointed to the north. Then an opened right hand would gently pat a closed left hand. Now both hands opened to each other, fingers outstretched. As Tom spoke, I remembered with fondness all those evenings, following dinner, when Susie would tell her stories.

Forty-five minutes into the story of Burnt Face, the great-grandkids were in their own dreamtime. David and I, however, were wide awake, animated by Tom's story and the deliberate movement of his arms and hands as he brought the story to life. Immediately following "Burnt Face," as if a natural continuation, came the story of Frank He Does It and his visit by the Little People. It was almost midnight when Tom decided to "call it a night," and David picked up his daughter, Tessa, and carried her to bed.

Stories are told all the time, any place—prior to a sweat bath, following a meal, at a powwow, during a tribal council meeting, at a basketball game. Perhaps some folks have just arrived for an evening visit, the coffee is heated up and served, "it's the Indian way," and someone asks for a particular story. It might be that the story comes while on a drive to town. Each time Tom and I would drive down to Crow Agency or over to Billings, there would be some gully, perhaps a ridge, or maybe a rock outcropping, or an Eagle would be spotted flying above, and a story would come forth. It might be an abbreviated story of Old Man Coyote, or it could be a tale of early Crow history: "We used to have horse races there, and. . . ." It might be a medicine story:

And as he drove past those rocks there, something caught his eye. He couldn't make it out. So he parked his pickup along the shoulder of the road and walked up over, on the other side, of those rocks there. And there, on the other side, was an Eagle, . . . just like the one seen at this place in that dream I told you about.

Most of all, for Tom, or Lawrence Aripa or Mari Watters, or for all who continue telling the stories, there was and is no greater love than sharing them with the children, at home or in the schools. Lawrence is always in demand by teachers at the reservation schools as well as at schools throughout northern Idaho and eastern Washington. To give further meaning to his stories, Lawrence often brings in various art objects—his grandmother's beaded bag, his own feathered headdress and dance roach. The care with which he tells his stories is reflected in the care Lawrence takes in removing and returning these "priceless things" from and to their storage case. Each article has its own special wrapping and place within the case. When a fourth grader asks him why he tells his stories, Lawrence says, "It's like getting coups; it's the greatest honor for me personally." "The stories were handed to my grandfather," Lawrence says, "and now I hand them to the children. The stories are our textbooks; they teach and our children need these stories." As Tom Yellowtail once said to me, "If all those great stories were told, . . . great stories will come!"

Purposes of Oral Literature
Integration
The world traveled is a world mythically endowed, brought forth in the adventures of Coyote and the other myth people. But it is a world not always readily apparent or accessible. The challenge for human peoples, as stated by Vic Charlo, is to "claim the linkage. "Human peoples seek that which mythic peoples have established and continue to nurture—a world that offers meaning and guidance, a world that offers the spiritual power to animate it all. Not to claim that linkage results in loss and estrangement, in what is feared most, ostracization, results in "death."

For Charlo as well as other Inland Peoples, it is in the oral literature that the mythic world of Coyote is made immediate and accessible, that the linkage is claimed.[1] The various cultural themes and literary motifs—the "what"—and the special qualities of orality, the techniques of the storyteller and the power in words—the "how"—all coalesce, bringing the listener into the world of story as a *participant*. In turn, the world entered through story becomes the world then traveled throughout one's life. The world of myth and the world of experience are one and the same, if the linkage is claimed.

One of the primary purposes of the oral literature is the integration of the human with the world. As alluded to by Mary Eyley, a Cowlitz storyteller, the stories are like canoes, you untie them when you start out, are told to stay on course when you wander off, and then tie the myth up when you finish for the night.[2] You travel via the vehicle of your story. A similar idea was shared with me by Vic Charlo. "The stories are what we have to explore with," he said. Certainly in the act of storytelling, the listeners as participants are integrated into the story as they run with Coyote and feel the splash of water, as they themselves contribute to the paddling of the canoe through the rivers of the mythic landscape. As the words are uttered and the ée's are heard, the story is vitalized by the participation of its members.

But the explorations of the canoe vitalize much more. The canoeing, in fact, continues outside the telling. When Coyote's territory is intimately explored, its mythic meanings and powers are renewed in the individual and brought forth into the experiential world. Ontological, aesthetic, and ethical as well as pragmatic meanings are applied to the various ambiguities and dilemmas encountered by men and women in everyday living. Family and kinship are made whole. In Basil White's story, "The Animals and the Sea Monster," the world of the Kootenai is named, "for the humans that's going to settle down, so they know where they are

. . ." Humanity is vitalized by the participation of its members.

Not only is the world of human peoples rendered meaningful and animated, but each time the canoe is launched and the world explored, all "peoples"—animal, plant, stone, and water—are affected. The animals— Grizzly Bear, Rattlesnake, Muskrat—go to the mountains, the birds—Swallows—to the sky, and the fishes— Salmon—to the rivers. As wonderfully exemplified in Basil White's story, an entire landscape is named and made. The Magpie and Woodpecker brothers are to be seen near Libby, Montana; Little Heart is found along the Kootenai River; and near Nelson, the Sea Monster's big tunnel and footprint are seen. In the speaking, the animals, the rivers, and the land are brought forth and are given their particular characteristics. In the telling, the relationships between animal and human and spirit are kept in balance and the world is made whole. Through the participation of all its members, the world is vitalized. All linkages are claimed.

Education

In addition to it role in integrating humans and their world, oral literature fills a critical didactic function. Moral lessons and practical information are offered. The basic values of humanity and the cosmos—what has been, what is, what can be, and what should be— are all enshrined in the oral literature and explored in the telling. As Vic Charlo has said, "The stories are what we have to explore with." From the stories, the knowledge of right and wrong, as well as the practical knowledge of how to live in this certain place, is imparted.

It is Coyote and the Elk who establish how a hunter is to respect the animal he hunts: "Nothing will they throw away," "you must not be proud," "you must not kill too many of any kind of animal." The story of Burnt Face illustrates the importance of self-sacrifice, gift giving, and reciprocity. Among the Crow, the peculiar antics of an individual are often explained in terms of Old Man Coyote, as if that behavior is modeled after the trickster's example. As a friend once said to me, "We don't just talk about Coyote, we do Coyote!" We can see the trickster vividly portrayed in the deception perpetrated by Wise Man. Among the Sanpoil, the Coyote narratives provide the guidelines and structure for one of their most important ceremonies, the First Salmon Ceremony.[3] Coyote's actions explain the origin of the salmon, describe the traps used in catching the fish, tell of the preparations for serving the first salmon caught, explain the duties of the Salmon Chief, and even tell how to care for the bones of the salmon, once the flesh is eaten. It is Sweat Lodge himself who shows why and how the sweat bath is to be used. In "Burnt Face" is found the archetype for the vision quest or any rite of passage. Myths provide a guide for living.

While many stories are told in the company of adults, they are meant for people of all ages. Indeed some stories are intended specifically for children—the Mosquito story told by the Kootenai, for example.[4] Lawrence Aripa remembers being told as a child the story of Cosechin, a man who has "no respect for anything" and pays the consequences by being banished. Every time Lawrence did something wrong, "I was always bad to my brothers and sisters," his grandfather would call him Cosechin and would retell the story, and then ask, "Do you want to disappear just like Cosechin?"

Because the stories are so richly layered with symbolic meanings, literary motifs, and moral lessons, the oral literature speaks to everyone. Each winter season, as the same story cycles are retold by the elders, new life experiences and advanced maturity yield new meanings for their listeners. Basic teachings are offered, new insights are obtained, and essential values are reiterated for young and old alike.

This is not to suggest that the stories are told for explicitly moralistic reasons. The telling of a particular story is not typically followed by a specific, Aesoplike, "moralistic-commentary."[5] The stories are never analyzed or talked about in that way. Moral lessons are deeply embedded within the narratives, to be sure, but they are left to be discovered and explored by the listener. The great truths in life are to be actively sought out.

Entertainment

Another purpose of oral literature is to entertain by providing a sense of drama, of suspense, of humor, a coloring to the mundane, a tone to life. People cry and laugh through the stories. A people's stories provide an opportunity to "lighten the load," as Vic Charlo puts it. Experiencing the outrageous antics of Coyote can certainly bring a smile, perhaps a laugh. There is a certain delight in the notion of Frog outracing Antelope! As Archie Phinney, a Nez Perce, observed, "Humor is undoubtedly the deepest and most vivid element in this mythology, the element that animates all the pathos, all the commonplace and the tragic, the element that is most wasted by transliteration.[6]

According to Charlo, laughter also allows you to "explore the heavy issues," just like during the "heavy moments" of an important ceremony when the elders light up a cigarette and "say outrageous things!" The laughter from the stories highlights and allows access to the critical lessons and vital issues to be faced in life.

Explanation

I should note my reluctance to isolate as a primary role of the stories an "explanatory" purpose per se. As popularly alluded to, such a position holds that myths and tales are "created" by a people to help offer explanations for why and how the world operates, to solve life's troubling mysteries. My reluctance to join that school stems from two concerns: First, there is a tendency when proposing an explanatory function for these stories to juxtapose and compare myth with scientific enquiry. "Myths are simply ill-founded, early attempts to explain what would be understood by an informed science." In this line of thinking, myth is too easily relegated to a position of a "prescience" or a "false science," to quaint belief, fantasy, and illusion. As previously mentioned, the truth of myth is expressed metaphorically and anagogically as opposed to empirically and thus scientifically. And second, to suggest an explanatory function presupposes a world view in which there is a reality separate from that of story: "Myths account for the world." Such a dichotomy is inconsistent with the cultural theme of kinship and connectedness, and with the understandings that the "stories make the world" and that the "world is the story." Nevertheless, this is not to suggest that explanatory elements are not occasionally expressed in the telling. Indeed, this has become even more pronounced with the Euro-Americanization of some of the stories and as these stories are told in a non-Indian school setting. "And . . that's . . why . . Coeur d'Alene Lake . . is *blue!*" But it is one thing to tell a story to explain why Coeur d'Alene Lake is *blue*, and quite another to name, bring forth, and participate in the *blue* of Lake Coeur d'Alene through the telling of that story. "And here's the Rock . . , all blue, just a rollen, just *mad*. And he goes, he goes over the cliff, *down* he goes. And he *rolls* and *rolls*. He goes into the lake . . ."

So why are the stories told and to whom are they told? They are told in order to *integrate,* to *educate,* and to *entertain* all the peoples. The children and the adults of the human, animal, and mythic peoples all depend on the telling of the myths and tales, for within the stories are what is essential and meaningful, what is real. As Barre Toelken and Tacheeni Scott so poignantly state with reference to the contrast between Euro-American and Navajo narrative performances, Euro-American "audiences are said to *suspend disbelief* in watching a play, while Navajos can be said to *intensify their sense of reality* by watching Ma'i" (Coyote).[7] In like fashion, the stories of the Inland Peoples intensify and bring forth the world, integrating and vitalizing all the peoples—human, animal, Elk, Coyote, Sweat Lodge—and the world—rivers, lakes, mountain ridges—within and through the stories. From the stories, the world is made. "If all those great stories were told, . . . great stories will come!"

|

COSECHIN

Lawrence Aripa, Coeur d'Alene[8]

Cosechin was one of our . . ancestors,
    and he lived way up at the mouth . . of the St. Joe
        where it is very small yet,
            he was a *me-e-an, me-e-an* man.
He hated everything.
He would do anything to hurt people,
    he'd live by himself,
        he was just *cruel* . . . to animals.
He would knock down trees
    and not use them.
He would grab leaves from the trees in the springtime
    and scatter them *to* try to *kill* the trees.
And you know it's the custom of the Indian that when they're going to use something from a tree
    or . . even fish or hunt,
        they . . ask permission first . . .
            "Mr. Tree may I use some part of you
                or I need it . . for warmth for my children,"
    and that type of thing.
Well he didn't think that way.
He was just mean,
    no good.

He'd even . . go to bed, go to sleep at night
    and he'd lay along the bank . . of the river
        and he'd have . . a rawhide rope that tied across . . the water.
And if anybody came up at night in a canoe
    or tried to get by,
        he'd just start shooting with his bow and arrow
            no matter who it was.

And so . . he was, he was just . . *mean*
    just awful.

And so . . the people would go and tell him,
    "Please take it easy,
        try, try and have patience
            try and be kind to the animals
                to your . . neighbors."
And he'd just say
    "Heck with it
        I don't have to."
He'd say
    "I am Co-o-sechin (slow deliberate voice)
        and I'm going to take care of myself
            and heck with everybody." . .

And then . . . one day they got together.
And so they called him
    and they brought him in front of their . . council.
And they told him, . . .
    "You tell us that you . . are above all of us,
        You look down at us.
            We are nothing compared to you.
              You hate everything . .
    Alright, you said you could take care of yourself,
        but if . . you do one . . more . . bad . . thing,
            we are going to . . *get rid* of you.
    We won't kill you yet,
        but we will kill you later . . if you don't . . change.
    So what we will do is we will *banish you*,
        we will turn you loose in the mountains
            let you . . take care of yourself
              and let's see how far you can go by yourself."
And so . . he thought about it . . .
And he thought. . . . (long deliberate pause)
    "They are *right*! . .
        I can't live out there . . by myself.
        I have to depend on others."

So he did change . . .

So . . . they . . . thought it was funny . . . when they saw him petting a dog,
    petting a horse
        talking to people,
            telling stories to children . . .
And . . he was just. . . . completely *different*! . .
And they couldn't . . couldn't believe it!

And then . . all of a sudden . . without any warning . . .
    he went back to his old ways like.
And then . . all of a sudden . . he disappeared . . .
And . . for years and years . . they've said,
    "Somebody *killed* him!" . .
And others says
    "No . . . he just *ran* off."
And others says
    "No! . . . he . . . he just . . got *chewed up* by something,
        something killed him,
    No."
And so . . for years and years . . nobody knew.
Nobody *ever did* find out about what happened to Cosechin! . .

ELK AND THE YOUNG MAN
ANONYMOUS WASCO[9]

There was a man at Dog River,[10]
    in days gone by,
        whose wife was with child.
Pretty soon she gave birth to the child.
While she was sick,
    he carried wood,
        and one day a piece of bark fell on his forehead
            and cut him.

When the boy was large enough to shoot,
    he killed birds and squirrels.

He was a good shot.

One day the father said,
    "You don't do as I used to.
        I am ashamed to own you.
    When I was of your age,
        I used to catch young elks.
    One day when I caught a young one,
        the old elk attacked me,
            and made the scar you see on my forehead."

The boy had a visit from an Elk.
And the Elk said,
    "If you will serve me and hear what I say,
        I will be your helper,
            and will help you in every necessity.
    You must not be proud.
    You must not kill too many of any kind of animal.
    I will be your guardian spirit."

The young man became a great hunter,
    knew where every animal was,
        bear,
            elk,
                deer.
He killed what he needed for himself,
    and no more.

The old man, his father, said,
    "You are not doing enough.
        At your age I used to do more."
The young man was grieved at his father's scolding.

The Elk,
    the young man's helper,
        was very angry at the old man.
But at last she helped the young man to kill five herds of elk.
The young man killed all except his own Elk,
    though he tried to kill even her.

This Elk went to a lake and pretended to be dead.

The young man went into the water to draw the Elk out,
    but as soon as he touched it,
        both sank.

After touching bottom,
    the young man woke as from a sleep,
        and saw bears,
            deer,
                and elks without number,
        and they were all persons.
Those that he had killed were there too,
    and they groaned.
A voice called,
    "Draw him in." [five times]
Each time the voice was heard,
    he was drawn nearer his guardian spirit, the Elk,
        till he was at her side.

Then the great Elk said,
    "Why did you go beyond what I commanded?
        Your father required more of you than he himself ever did.
    Do you see our people on both sides?
        These are they whom you have killed.
            You have inflicted many needless wounds on our people.
    Your father lied to you.
        He never saw my father,
            as he falsely told you,
                saying that my father had met him.
        He also said that my father gave him a scar.
            This is not true.
                He was carrying fire-wood when you were born,
                    and a piece of bark fell on him
                        and cut him.
        He has misled you.
    Now I shall leave you,
        and never be your guardian spirit again."

When the Elk had finished,
    a voice was heard saying five times,
        "Cast him out."

The young man went home.

The old man was talking,
      feeling well.

The young man told his two wives to fix a bed for him.
They did so.
He lay there five days and nights,
      and then told his wives,
            "Heat water to wash me,
                  also call my friends so that I may talk to them.
            Bring five elk-skins."
All this was done.

The people came together,
      and he told them,
            "My father was dissatisfied because,
                  as he said,
                        I did not do as he had done.
            What my father wanted grieved the guardian spirit which
            visited me
                  and aided me.
            My father deceived me.
                  He said that he had been scarred on the head by an Elk
                  while taking the young away.
                  He said that I was a disgrace to him.
                  He wanted me to kill more than was needed.
            The spirit has left me,
                  and I die."

|

FROG AND ANTELOPE
BARNABY, KOOTENAI[11]

Well, I'll tell you how,
      long ago,
            Frog won over Antelope.

There was a town.
It was named Fish Hawk Nest.[12]

Antelope was chief.
Antelope runs fast.
Even the best runners were beaten by Antelope.
He was a powerful spirit person,
    and won over everybody.

There was a town of Frogs.
Then Chief Frog thought,
    "I'll cheat Antelope."
He said to his tribe,
    "Let us play with Antelope!"
They said to him,
    "What shall we do with Antelope?
        He runs fast."
He said to them,
    "We shall go,
        all of us.
    We shall play with him."
Then he told his people what to do.
All the Frogs said,
    "Well, your thoughts are good."
That chief said,
    "I'll go alone.
        Later on,
            if he agrees,
        tomorrow we shall go."
The Frogs said,
    "It is well."
Then he started.

When he arrived at Antelope's lodge,
    Antelope said to Frog,
        "Why do you come to my lodge?"
Frog said,
    "I came here to see if you are not afraid to run a race with me."
Antelope laughed.
He thought,
    "Even if he runs fast,
        I can easily beat Frog."
Frog was told,

"If you agree,
  your property shall be my property.
You will pay it to me."
Frog said,
  "Go.
    I am glad.
  I'll take your property."
Then they laughed at him because he thought he could beat Antelope.
Frog said,
  "Tomorrow just at noon I'll come,
    accompanied by my tribe."
Then Frog started off.

When he came home,
  he said to his tribe,
    "Now we will beat Antelope and his children."
On the following morning the Frogs started,
  all of them.
There were many.
The women went along with the men Frogs.

When they almost came to the town,
  the chief said,
    "Before any one comes out,
      go and lie down along the trail.
    Go at a distance equal to a jump!
      You shall be a jump apart."
Then the Frogs went to the starting place,
  and all of them lay down along the way they were to run.
They lay down up to the point where the track turned.
When this was done,
  others went to the town.

They said,
  "The Frogs have come to play with us."
Then all of them went out.
They went to the starting place.

Then the Frogs bet their property.
All their clothing was blue.

Then they bet with them.
They asked much,
    because they thought the Frogs would be beaten.
They thought they themselves would win.
This is what they spoke among themselves.

Then Antelope stood up.
He laughed at his enemy.
Frog was laying there.
Then he looked at Antelope.

They said,
    "Now start!"
Then Frog jumped up.
Antelope laughed.
His enemy looked funny to him.

Antelope did not run fast when Frog gave his first jump.
Then another Frog lay there and jumped,
    and all the Frogs did so.
Then Antelope did not go very fast.
He had not gone far when he was left behind.

He ran fast,
    but even when he ran fast,
        the Frogs were ahead of him.
Then he arrived at the turning place,
    and when he got there,
        the Frogs lay down in the opposite direction.
Then Antelope turned back,
    but the Frogs were always ahead of him.

Then Antelope tired hard.
He knew that he would be beaten.
Antelope was not yet near the starting point when Frog arrived.

Then all laughed,
    but the people were sick at heart,
        because Frog had won.
They looked at Frog.

He was not out of breath,
        because he had just given one jump,
                and then had not moved any more.
He just jumped back from there.
Therefore he was not out of breath,
        but Antelope was puffing.
He lay on his back,
        and he said,
                "You beat me, Frog."

Then Frog took what he had won.
He went back,
        and those who lay down did not move.
In the evening they went back,
        and it was heard by all that Frog had beaten Antelope.

Now I have told how Frog beat Antelope in olden days.

|

TWO COYOTES
HARRY WHEELER, NEZ PERCE[13]

One more story which is wonderful,
        true,
                and funny.

Two coyotes went up the river
        and they came to a big bench
                and from there they saw people living below,
                        near the river.
And the two friends said to each other,
        "You go ahead."
Then one said,
        "No.
                You go."
And the other said,
        "No."
And for a long time they argued,

they contested.

Then one said,
    "Then you go first.
        They will see you soon
           and they will say,
               'That coyote is going on the trail.'"
"I am not a coyote." [the second coyote said]
"But you are the same as I am. [the first coyote said]
    We are the same in every way
        and we are both coyotes."
"No. [the second coyote said]
    I am 'another one.'"
Thus they contested.

Then one said, [the second coyote]
    "Now you go first."
There was a ridge on which the people from below could see everything.
When he walked on, [the first coyote]
    he went on,
        went over a small ridge,
           the people below said to each other,
               "That coyote is going upstream."
And they came out [the people]
    and watched the coyote going.

"See," he said to his friend, [the first coyote]
    "what did they say?
        You are a coyote."
"Then you come too," he said, [the first coyote]
    "and they are going to say the same of you.
        You are a coyote."
"Alright, I'll go," [the second coyote said]
    and he slowly started walking on the trail from there.
Then [the people said]
    "Ah, another one again,
        another one again."
Then he came, [the second coyote]
    "See, I am not a coyote.
        I am 'another one.'

See, the people said that I am 'another one.'"

That's all.

|

COYOTE AND THE WOMAN
Lawrence Aripa, Coeur d'Alene[14]

One time, . .
    a long time ago, . . .
        the Coyote . . was out enjoying himself, . .
            and he was . . running up the Spokane River, . .
                really having fun . .
He was running in the . . *sand*
    on the rocks,
        and just enjoying himself,
            really having a good time . . .

And all of a sudden . . he stops, . .
    and he sees a camp . . .
And there are tipis
    and smoke
        and people *all* over . .
And he looked, . .
    and on the shore . . there was a group of . . people . .
Some were fishing.
Some were cleaning fish . .
And he watched.
And as he watched,
    he saw them,
        really busy
            cleaning a *lot* of fish
They were preparing for the winter.
So they had a *lot* of fish that they were cleaning . .

And as they cleaned
    there was . . one young lady . . that stood out . .
The Coyote kept looking at her.
And as he looked he says,

"Oh my gosh . . that is the most beautiful creature that I have ever
        seen!" . .
And as he watches, . .
        the other women and the men . . are all singing.
They are singing because they are happy that they have enough fish . . for the
winter . . .
They come here every year to *fish*
        and get a lot of fish for the winter . . .
And so they were happy,
        as they sang,
                and as they worked . . .

And the Coyote,
        he couldn't keep his eyes off this beautiful creature . . .
He kept watching her,
        her movements were something . . were something to look at.
And he just kept watching her,
        and watching.

And finally he couldn't stand it anymore . . .
So he runs into the camp, . .
        and he asks for the chief . . .
And he tells the chief, . .
        "I have seen the most beautiful woman that I have ever . . set my eyes
        on, . .
                and I want her . . .
        I want her to be mine forever!" . .
The chief looked at him with a surprised look
        and he started to laugh . . .
And then . . the Coyote says,
        "What are you laughing at?
        What is so funny?" . .
The chief says,
        "You are a *coyote*!
                You are not *human* . . .
        You can't take care of a human being.
        You are only a *coyote*!" . .
And the Coyote says,
        "Well, . . what I can do is

I can . . *dance*
                and I can pray
                        and the Great Animal Spirit . . will change me . . .
        He will change me into a handsome . . *man*."
But the chief says
        "*No-o-ho . . no-o!*"
He says, . .
        "You know,
                I know,
                        and my daughter knows, . .
                                that you are a *coyote* . . .
        You'll *always* be a coyote.
                And . . *no* that can't happen!"
So he says,
        "No,
                you get out.
        Leave this camp.
                Don't bother us." . .

So the Coyote left the camp.
But he was angry . . .
And he says,
        "I have to have that woman.
                I have to have her." . .
He says,
        "I will get the help from *another* tribe." . .

So he goes to the Kalispel . . .
And he tells the Kalispel, . .
        "You people . . you fish on the river, . .
                and you get salmon."
And the Kalispel chief says,
        "Yes we do.
        We go there
                and we join the . . Spokanes,
                        and the Coeur d'Alenes,
        and we all get salmon
        There is enough salmon for everybody."
And the Coyote says

"Well, . . I want to ask a favor . . .
I will bring you *more* salmon if you will help me.
Go and talk to the Coeur d'Alene chief, . .
  and tell him to let me have his daughter,
   let me have that beautiful creature."
And the Kalispel chief started to laugh.
He laughed and laughed.
And the Coyote says
 "What are you laughing about?". .
And he says
 "You are a *coyote*!
  You can't marry a human!"
And the Coyote says
 "I will change myself to a handsome . . man!"
And then the Kalispel chief says, . .
 "*Well* I will *know* that you are a coyote.
  You'll *always* be a coyote.
 No, . . I won't help you."

So he goes to the Spokane tribe . . .
And he tells the Spokane chief,
 "You fish out of the same river as the Kalispel
  and the Coeur d'Alene . . .
 You get a lot of salmon . . .
 If you will help me
  I will get you more salmon!" . .
And so the chief says
 "Well how can you do that?"
And he says
 "I have the power,
  and I can do it." . .
And he says
 "All I want you to do is *help* me." . .
And the Spokane chief says
 "What is it you want?" . .
He says
 "I want that *woman*.
 I want that beautiful woman as my mate." . .
And the Spokane chief . . began to laugh . .

He laughed and he laughed.
And the Coyote got angry.

And other . . people from the council *came* in.
And the Spokane chief told them what the Coyote had said,
    and *they* started to laugh.
They laugh and laugh.
And he left the camp while they were still laughing . . .

And so . . he says
    "I will teach them.
        I will teach them a lesson . .
    They can't laugh at me."
He says
    "That isn't right.
    But I'm going to have that woman." . .

So he goes
    and he starts *praying*
        and he *dances*
            and then . . he asks for the Great Animal Spirit . .
All of a sudden the Animal Spirit appears,
    and he says
        "Yes, . . what is it?". .
And the Coyote says, . .
    "You owe me a favor, . .
        and I am asking for it now." . .
And so . . the Animal Spirit says
    "*What* is it?" . .
He says
    "I want you to give me . . the power of *strength* . . .
    I want to be *strong*,
        and be able to . . move about . . in the *air*
            and everything." . .
And so the Animal Spirit didn't know what it was for.
So he says
    "Yes, . . you can." . .

And so . . the Coyote . . . went to the *rocks*
    he went to the mountains

He got big rocks, . .
      he got mud, . .
          dirt, . .
              little rocks.
And he moved them *all* to the river . . .
He pushed them into the river,
      and by doing that he created . . *falls*, . .
          he created Spokane Falls,
              Post Falls.
He created other *streams*,
      that run away from the river . . .

And then . . he went back to the . . Coeur d'Alene chief . . .
And he says
      "There are no more salmon coming up that river . . .
      And the only way to can get salmon again . . is to let me have your
      daughter." . .
And the Coeur d'Alene chief says
      "N-o-o! . .
      It is not possible
          and I will not do it!" . .
And so . . the Coyote says
      "Well, . . you will not have any salmon . . .
      You will no longer have salmon until . . you tell me I can have her,
          then I will let the salmon come back up again.
      Otherwise . . you will not get salmon." . .

And as he started to leave
      a young man
          who had been . . more or less courting the young lady
              he too was a very important man,
                  he was part of the chief's line,
      and so he followed the Coyote . . .

And so . . the Coeur d'Alene chief . . waited and waited.
He says,
      "He will not . . keep the fish from us
      We will get it." . .
But there was no sign of the Coyote . .
And the Chief says

"When he comes back
        we will tell him no
We can't do it." . .

And then the people started to talk . . .
        "We have no fish.
        The fish stopped coming . . .
        We need *more* fish, . .
                and we must get it." . .
So the chief says
        "Well, . . the next time the Coyote comes back
                then we will talk.
        And maybe something can be worked out." . .

But they waited, . .
        and waited . . .
And the young man
        who had been *courting* . . the lady . .
                never said anything
                        but he was glad
He was walking around *smiling*
        and dancing
                and being *happy* . . .

And all of a sudden word came
        they found the Coyote.
He was dead . . .

And so the spell was never taken away . . .
And to this day, . .
        the Coeur d'Alenes,
                the Spokanes,
                        the Kalispels,
                                the Colvilles,
                                        we . . have . . no . . *salmon* . . .
The Coyote never came back.
And he never broke the spell.
So ever since then . . . we have no more salmon. . . .

Post Falls on the Spokane River, northern Idaho. (Courtesy of the Idaho State Historical Society)

THE ANIMALS AND THE SEA MONSTER

BASIL WHITE, KOOTENAI[15]

Long ago, . . .
    when the earth was, . .
        beginning of the earth here, . .
            there was no *humans*. . . . (in a very slow pace and deliber-
            ate voice throughout)
There was just . . *animals,* . .
    they talked just like we *do,*
        they talked to each *other.* . . .
So-o one day . . . they got together
and . . . they told each other,
        they says, . .
            "We heard, . .
                one day . . they're going to . . put humans on this
                earth . . .
            So-o . . is there *anything* we can do . . about it?" . .
Another animal got up
    and says,
        "Wel-l-l, . . . if there're going to be humans, . .
        let there be *humans* . . .
    Let the humans come into this world. . . . .
    We can . . *rule* this world,
        we can *rule* the *humans.*" . . .
Another animal got up
    and he says,
        "No-o, . . we're not going to do that.
    Just let them be." . .

S-o-o the story I want to tell you is . . is about . . . the village, . .
    somewheres, . .
        someplace, . .
            with all kind of . . animals living together . . .

One day,
    one hunter,
        one . . hunter come back in, . .

and . . crying,
   he says,
        "There's a . . *woman* . . laying in the woods . . *dead*, . .
           with an *arrow* sticking through her . . . belly." . . .
So everybody gathered around,
   they went over
      and . . looked at the woman. . . .
Sure enough . . she was dead . . .
They took the arrow out
   and they couldn't identify the *arrow*, . .
      they don't know where the *arrow* come from. . . .
Well he went round and round,
   asking everybody, . .
      elders, . .
         and . . . anybody that's *wise* . . .
They still couldn't find out where the . . arrow come from . . .

In the meantime, . .
   over in his hut, .
      there was a . . *Muskrat.* . . .
You know,
   sometime when you look at him . . you think he have no *eyes*,
      but they do-o-o, .
         they do have eyes . . .
So . . that's what he done to *himself* . .
Well he was the *guilty one*, .
   he was the one who *killed* this woman . . .
So he went back, . .
   mashed up his face . . with a rock . . .

So he was in *bed*, .
   when all the peoples, .
      all the other animals got around him, . .
         got around his hut . . .
So his . . . his *grandma* was . . a *Frog* . . .
So the other people, .
   the other animals asked the Frog,
      he says,
         "*Where is* . . . *where is* Muskrat?" . .

He says,
    "Oh, he's in bed,
        he's sick . . .
    You can't go in there . . .
    He's *very* sick." . .
And the animals say,
    "Well . . . we want to *talk* to him . . .
    We want to find out where that *arrow* come from that killed that
    woman." . .
Frog says,
    "Okay,
        you can go in, . .
            ask him." . .

The chief walked in
    and . . . asked him, . .
        and told him,
            "Then you *talk!*"
He shook his head . .
He says,
    "*No!*" . . .
"Can you identify . . the *arrow* for us?" . . . .
And he just held out his hand . .
    and he says,
        "Give it to me."
And he *give it* to him . . .
He kinda sniff-ed around,
    and he couldn't *mo-v-v-e*, . .
        very well *move around* . . .
So all he done was just . . . put his eyes up and down . . .
And then what the other . . animals . . thought . . . he was saying . . .
    "He says, . .
        'It come from *up above* . . .
        The *arrow* come from up above.'" . .

So everybody put on their . . . stuff,
    gathered their arrows, . .
        their tomahawks, . .
            their whatnot . .

whatever they used . . to go to *war.*
"We're going to declare *war* . . on the people . . *up above*." . .

So one of the animals says,
    "How are we going to get *up there?*"
And another one says,
    "Well I'm going to shoot an arrow up." . . . .
So this other,
    "Well how long will it *take?*" . .
"Oh,
    it will take about a day and a half!"

So the . . animals shot up an *arrow* . . up in the air . . .
They waited . . al-l-l that da-a-y . .
    and it took all day for the arrow to be felt . . up above . . .
So he . . says,
    "Okay, . .
        rest of you start sho-o-tin' . . your *arrows*." . .
And they all start sho-o-tin' their arrows up,
    and it formed into ladder . . .
And it come *all the way down* to the ground . . .

And . . . there was about . . oh about two three inches that was . . . short . . .
So they didn't know what . . what they were going to *use* to *hold up* the
ladder . . .
So he . . put a *ro-o-ck* underneath it . . .

In the meantime . . . there was a . . guy went over . . .
    and they told him, [to one of the warriors]
        "Are you *ready?*"
He says,
    "*No*,
        I'm not ready . . .
            I won't be able to be ready and do anything.
            I gotta go back, . . .
                put . . put my stuff away.
        It will take me about a day . .
        And I've got to do something else,
            that will take me *another* day . .

> *Then* I can come." . .

So he left. . . .

And so the chief says, . .
    the chief of the animals says,
        "Wel-l-l, . . .
            we can't wait *that* long." . .

So they a-a-ll . . . left . .
    they *a-a-ll* went up . .
        they start climbing that . . . ladder . . .

And when they got up there, . .
    they start walking . .
And sure enough, . .
    there was villages al-l-l over the place. . . . . .

So they . . they started . . they started a *wa-a-r* . . .
Every time they'd sho-o-o-t this . . .
    this guy would shoot *back* . .
        kept on shooting each other,
            shooting each other . . .

And then finally there was one . . wise . . old . . man. . . .
He says,
    "Just a *minute*. . . .
        You guys realize . .
            are you guys paying attention?
        You realize that . . our enemy, . .
            every time he shows up
                and shoots us, . .
                    he's a left-handed . . .
        He can't *al-l-l* be left-handed there." . .
And then this second chief turned around,
    and he says,
        "Well we'll have to look . . look into that." . .

So they went around again
    started shooting at each other again.
And *every time* there'd be only o-n-ne . . one enemy show up. . . . .

So finally . . . the second chief, . .

assistant chief, . .
>says,
>>"Ha-a-a,
>>>I know who it is.
>>>>Let's let him go-o.
>>>>>He's just trying to distract us." . . .

That was . . *Muskrat* . . .
As soon as everybody left, . .
>then he went up *too* . .
So he went ahead,
>and he got back into his . . . his playground up there . . .
So everybody says,
>"*Let* him go-o-o." . . (in a disappointed voice)
So they . . all . . went back.

And in the meantime, . .
>the guy who stayed behind, . .
>>when he got over to there, . .
>>>got back over to where everybody gathered . . to start up,
>>nobody was *there* . . .
And he got mad
>and he kicked that *ladder.*
And he kicked it down. . . . .
There was no ways of coming back down. . . . .

So when the warriors got back to the place where they were going to come back down
>there was no *ladder* . . .
He says,
>"How are we going to get down?"
They started asking each other,
>"How are we going to get . . back down?" . .
It's a long ways to jump! . . .
So one by one, . .
>they start jumping down. . . .

So when you cut open a fish, . .
>you see a little piece of meat on there. . . . (motioning with hands as if opening up a fish)
That's from . . when the fish jumped down, . .

The Animals and the Sea Monster / 201

they smashed up.
When they put them back together, . .
    there was one small piece . . that they couldn't *find*, . .
        so they had to put this little meat there in order to . . get them to
        go again. . . .

So then . . our brothers and sisters . .
    that's Magpie . .
        Woodpecker. . . .
            that's all these birds that fly . .
    got together.
They says,
    "Oh, . .
        we're not going to jump back down like what them other peoples
        are *doing* . . .
        We're going . . to go walk til we come to the *end*.
        That's where we're going . . to get back down." . .
So they did,
    they went off . . .

And at that time . . . there was *another* . . . animal coming around,
    coming along,
        a *Giant*,
            coming along the *Kootenai River* . . .
He was coming in from the Kootenay Lake, . .
    and he was on his way,
        he was . . crawling . . along the *river* there . . .
Well he was on his way
    and thes-s-e . . brothers
        Magpie
            and Woodpecker . . come back down . . . (from the sky)
Some of you peoples know this place, . .
    they call *Libby, Montana* right now . . .
And if you drive out of . . Libby, Montana there, . .
    about five miles out of Montana,
        you . . look up when you are going towards Kalispell, . .
        you look up in the . . mountain about five miles out . . up
        on the hillside,
            you'll see something, . . .
                all standing in a row . . .

Kootenai River near
Bonners Ferry, Idaho.

just straight on down like that,
they're standing in a row . . .
That's the . . . Magpie brothers, . .
    Woodpecker . . .

And in the meantime,
    that's when the . . *Giant* was crawling through there . . .
And Magpie, . .
    they all asked each other,
        "What is *he* doing?
            He never does wander around.
        What is he doing wandering around through here?" . . .
So they . . told each other,

The Animals and the Sea Monster / 203

"Well let's *ask* him."
So they . . turned around
      and asked him,
            "What are you . . doing crawling around? . .
                  You hardly *go around*?" . .
He says,
      "Well, . .
            we hear . . that they were going to put humans on this *earth* . . .
      They're going to start putting humans on this earth
            so. . . . the Great Spirit told me to go around,
                  start naming these places,
                        for the humans that's going to settle down,
                              so they know where they are." . . (laughter
                              from audience)
So these Woodpeckers got mad at him . . .
They told him,
      they says, . .
            "Open your mouth, . .
                  we're going to . . *feed you*." . .
"Okay." . .
So they . . . got a . . heart of a deer,
      a deer . . heart . . .
And so in the meantime they stuck a hot rock inside of that heart . . .
They were going to try to *kill* this Giant . .
So they says,
      "Okay, . .
            open your mouth." . .
Then he opens his mouth
      and looks up . . .
            and he *noticed* right away . . .
                  there is something *wrong* with that . . .
So he just . . give a *nod* to this heart that was . . coming down.
It went right beside him . . .
And then he *named* the place . . .
He said this place will be called
      Little Heart.

So he . . turns around
      and turns to Woodpecker
            and says,

"When you guys get back down to the river . . .
                  and if there happen to be a fish . . . *struggling*, . .
                     don't touch it." . . .

So they . . got back down to the river . . .
And the *first* thing he saw was a fish, . .
     going by . . struggling . . .
The oldest Magpie says,
     "Well, . .
          I'll be the one that's going to get it."
So the younger Magpie says,
     "No, . .
          I will."
He wouldn't listen to his brother . . .
He jumped in, . .
     and it was the . . Sea Monster's tongue, . .
          that swallowed him up . . .
And it took *all of them*, . .
     that's when he got angry . . .
He got *ang-r-y the-r-e*
     so . . the Monster took off . . .
Went back down to the Kootenay Lake . . .

Woodpecker
     and his family
          they all went down,
               his brothers,
                    and . . everybody went down to the Kootenay Lake,
                         all them birds,
                              and everyone . .
When they got down to the lake, . .
     he didn't find all the fish . . .

He says, . .
     "Killdeer, . .
          call in all the fish."
Killdeer bird, . .
     you know . . you see them going around the lake, . .
          you know . . you *look* at them the *way they do*, . .
               they kinda *dancing* around, . .

kinda *weave* back and forth . . .
So they're *calling* the fish out, . .
    to come on . . to come on the *land*, . .
        because there's going to be a big . . big party going on . . .
If it were *now* it would be a . . keg party . . . (big smile and laughter from audience)
All the fish come on the land . . .
"We got something for you . . .
    I want to ask you a few *questions*,
        you fish some *questions*." . .

So all the fishes got to the land
    and . . had a big feast there . . .
So all the fishes *got* there, . .
    all gathered around. . . .
And Magpie got up
    and he asked . . the fishes,
        he says, . .
            "Where is that Sea Monster hiding?" . . . .
Nobody would talk,
    none of the fish would talk.
They all . . . all sat there.
And he says,
    "You just wait, . . .
        someone else is coming." . . . .
So they waited and waited . . .

Finally this old man come out, ...
    this o-l-l-d a . . old fish,
        a sucker . . . *sucker* I think it is . . .
Got there
    and. . . . he . . he *give* him something to eat.
He says,
    "No, . . .
        I don't *eat* . . .
            All I do is *smoke*." . . .
So they give him . . some *smoke*.
He was smoking,
    and they asked him,
        they says,

"Where's the Sea Monster hiding?"
He says,
 "Every time I try to take a puff off this pipe, . .
  you watch my *eyebrows*, ...
   or my fore*head*." . . .
Every time he . . . takes a puff off hi-s-s a. . . . pipe, . .
 then you *watch* him . . .

He went along one side, . . .
 there was nothing
Come back
 and he take another puff.
And he went along *another* side, . .
 there's *nothing* there. . . .
On the third puff he took . . again,
 he looked up
  and right in the center of the lake there, . .
   that's a where he nodded . . .
That's where the *monster* is. . . . .

So the *Cran-n-e*,
 and all them long-legged. . . . animals went *out* there. . . .
Finally they stirred him up
 and. . . . took off on them . . .
And over . . in . . there just this side of Nelson[16]
 there's a big tunnel there . . .
  that's where the Sea Monster's home is.
He went back in there . . .

So-o there was no way they were going to get *him out*. . . . .
They says,
 "How are *we going* to get him out? . .
  Nobody knows how to get him out!" . .
Got on top of the end side
 and there was no way of . . . digging or anything . . .
If it were *now* there would be some peoples with *jackhammers*
 I guess they'd go *through* it . . . (laughter from audience)

And the Woodpecker started *pecking*. . . .
Finally he got *through* to him

Great blue heron.

    and nicked him, . .
        and took off again. . . . .
Took off
    and started to go out
And they told o-n-ne animal to stand by the main . . main a . . let out there, . .
    and try to *catch* him there.
And he *did*, . .
    stuck his a . . . spear, . .
        and they got him on a . . . on a back, . .
           they caught him there, . .
               and they hold him there . . .

For a long while they . . held him and held him . . .
Finally he left up his other leg, . .
    other . . part,
        you can see that over in *Nelson* too,
           on a big flat rock on the side
               there's a . . *great big* footprint on there . . .
That's that *Sea Monster's* footprint. . . .

And he . . gave a good yank

and he took off. . . .
And he starts going *around.* . . .
And all the w-a-a-y down, . .
     end of the lake
         and he starts *cutting* back in . . .
And if he did ever get through . . .
     he'd get up to Columbia, . .
         Windermere . .
            and then he'd cut around back to Cranbrook . .
               and then back to . . a . . Grasmere . .
                  back into . . Eureka . .
                     then back into Libby. .
                       and then he'd be going right around
                       this way again . . .[17]
So he was just going around in *circles.* . . .

So . . finally . . . they told one another,
     they says,
         "Send the word up ahead, . . .
            and there's a guy they call. . . . . Oneferd . . .
He *never* goes anywhere,
     that guy . . . (laughter from audience)
And he's *another* giant . . .
They got the *word* to him . . .
They *told* him,
     they says, . .
         "There's the Sea Monster coming,
            and he's going to try to make it through . . *your way.* . . .
         Is there any way . . that you . . can do to stop him?" . . . .
He says,
     "Well, . .
         I guess if there's a way I'll try."

So, . .
     some place along through there, . .
         you can see . . where there was a mountain,
            and part of it . . came down . . .
That was *his* work,
     he'd hit one side of the mountain,
         and then . . the other side, . .

The Animals and the Sea Monster / 209

and it got down there, . .
     and it built a *dike* like . . .

So the monster . . got there. . . .
    Well . . I guess it's about from here . . . to the . . first bench here . .
(indicating about fifteen feet wide)
     he almost got through. . . . again. . . . .
So they . . . *stopped* him alright,
    and he send the word back that he *stopped* him . . .

And *that's* when *Coyote* come in . . .
He told Coyote,
    "Well here . . . you take this hatchet, . . .
      go over there, . .
        and knock him on the head . . .
    No matter what he does,
     you just knock him on *the head*." . .

And he . . takes off . . .
Well . . they say at that time Coyote is the fastest *runner* . . .
So he *takes* off.
And he . . got there . . .
And that monster just . . turned around
    and looked at him,
      and he says,
        "Well . . I'm going to swallow you up!"
He jumped back . . .
He give a yip,
    and jumped back.
He says,
    "By god he almost *swallowed* me!" . .

And when . . *Fox* got there, . .
    Wolf got there, . .
      they says,
        "O-o-h . . we thought you were *something*, . .
        we depended on you . . .
        You can't even do *nothing*." . . . . (some light laughter from
the audience)

So . . *Wolf* got over there
   and . . . gave him a good . . whack on the head.
And they *killed* that *Sea Monster.* . . .

And they *cut* it open, . .
   they cut . . . his belly open, . .
      and they let all those other birds come out that was in there. . . .
That's how come you see, . .
   some of these birds you know that flies around,
      that some of you peoples do see it,
         they kind'a . .
            part of it is red, . .
               and part of it that's white . . .
   that's how come . . on account of . . them being inside the stomach of
   that *monster* so long. . . .

So . . . they says,
   "What are we going to do about the *Sea Monster?*
   What are we going to *do* with it?
   How are we going to get *rid* of it?" . . .
"Well,"
   they says,
      "We'll just have to wait for the chief to get here." . .
So they waited . . .

And then the chief got there,
   and they asked him,
      they says,
         "What are we going to do about this . . . Sea Monster?"
He says,
   "Well. . . . there's *always* a way, . .
   there's *always* a way to *do* things. . . . .
   First . . we're going to take this part,
      this part of the flesh here, . .
         which is white, . .
            cut a piece of it, . . .
               throw it *up* in the air
                  and that's for the *White* People." . .
That's how come the White Peoples are white,
   on account of . . the meat was white. . . .

Basil White, 1991.
(Photo by Jane Fritz)

They cut another piece of it off which is yellow.
They *threwed* it up.
That's for the *Oriental* People . . .

And they come to this little black . . . piece.
Threw it.
That's for the *Colored* People . . .

And he kept on doing it,
     kept on . . praying and praying,
          and. . . . different kind of nationalities. . . .
So it was *all over* . . .

They all stood around . . .
They says,
    "Well . . where does the *Indians* come from? . .
        Where will the *Indian* come from?" . .
"Oh . . we forgot all about *that*."
So there was just . . *dried-up* . . *blood* . . on the ground laying, . . .
    covered with grass.
So they just . . . rolled it in that grass
    and throw it up
        and that's the *Indians* . .
So that's how come the Indians are red. . . . (laughter from audience)

So . . there you are, . .
    that's the story I was told long long ago. . . .
So I'm glad you peoples came down to listen to me, . . .
    real nice. . . . . . .

Conclusion

You have, I hope, felt some of the interior of the tin shed. You are now familiar with some of the dominant and pervasive cultural themes and literary motifs of the Inland Peoples. It is the world of Old Man Coyote, Little Head, and Burnt Face, a world that offers kinship, guidance, and the power of life itself. We have reviewed some of the implications of orality, discussed many of the storytelling techniques used by raconteurs, and introduced the notion that the spoken word can affect the world. The telling of Coyote's stories, in fact, "makes the world."

Some essential questions are thus raised. How can the world abound with meaning and yet be brought forth by the words of a story? Is the world to be discovered? Or is the world to be formed? Does the world have existence? Or is it in need of existence? The answers lie in the story itself. For *the world is the story*! The story at once reveals discovery of that which was established by Coyote, thus allowing discovery of the transcendent archetypes within the world. Yet in the act of telling the story, the journey of Coyote is continued, bringing forth, forming, and manifesting those archetypes in the phenomenal world. The world is made and rendered meaningful in the act of revealing Coyote's stories of the world.

In telling the stories, the human peoples "claim linkage" with the world about them, with the animal peoples of the forests and the myth peoples of creation time. It is a world participated in.

St. Joe River, northern Idaho.

To participate in the stories, as suggested by Mary Eyley, is indeed to journey in a canoe. Within the story, you travel a mythic territory that unfolds before your eyes as the words of the story and the technique of the storyteller bring forth that world. It is an intimate and experiential journey.

Today two distinct types of canoes travel the waterways of the landscape. The newer canoe is outfitted with an outboard motor and covered with a thick glass pane. Within this canoe, you continue to observe a landscape rich in character; Coyote can still be seen running along the river's bank. But it is a landscape observed, not felt. You no longer need to paddle the canoe; you no longer feel the splash of the cold water; no ée's are voiced. You no longer participate in the story and with the mythic world. This canoe is the book, like the one you now hold in your hands; it's the canoe powered by the technology of literacy.

But if the canoe is to continue to travel the mythic landscape and the splash of the water is to be felt, the stories must go beyond literacy. Participation must not be mediated by the written word alone. To read from the pages of a book, as with memorization, is "too rigid." An element of spontaneity and immediacy necessary to draw the listeners into the story is lost. Along with the storyteller, the listeners must become participants, and each must contribute to the paddling of the canoe. A hand gesture, a facial expression, a look off in the distance not only reveals something of Coyote, but the emphasis placed in each gesture by the storyteller "speaks" to each individual listener. Should someone begin to "drift off," the storyteller can encourage his or her participation with added emphasis and gesturing. To look into the eyes of the listeners is to know to what extent each is paddling the canoe. While the literary motifs and the cultural themes of the narrative, the text, may remain consistent each time the story is told—indeed, should remain true to Coyote's story—the storyteller and the participants invigorate the telling, and the texture with its own distinct dynamic. The story is brought to life one more time. In the telling, Coyote is released to run along the river's bank and among the people. The eyes of the storyteller look into the eyes of the members of the story; in that re-membering, the characters of the story, no longer anchored to the page, beckon to the participants of that story.

Cliff SiJohn perhaps best expressed what it is to re-member when he said to me, "Watch and you'll see the storyteller become the Coyote!" While showing the teachers of the Coeur d'Alene school district how to tell these stories to their students, Cliff summed it up this way: "When you tell the stories, you've gotta go inside and become the Coyote, or the Bear, or the Mole. Feel it as they feel it. And tell the stories with your heart [gently patting himself on his chest], not up here [pointing to his head]. If you tell it with your heart, you'll have clean hands."

When you run with the Coyote, the story has been re-membered, the canoe has been launched. You've gone inside and participated; you've claimed the linkages.

I

Interpreting A Text

*T*o *illustrate more completely* the transcription process and illuminate many of the subtle yet significant features of the oral literature, let's revisit the
Crow story, "The Couple Befriended by the Moon."
This particular narrative, based upon Young Crane's
telling of the story in Apsáalooke (the Crow language)
some eighty years ago, was recorded by Robert Lowie,
who subsequently translated the story into English.[1]
What we have available in written form is a fairly
literal transcription of the words used in the original
telling. The phrasing and structuring are thus intact.
To preview some of Lowie's original transcription, several verses, comprising the first two scenes, are repro-
duced here, both in Apsáalooke and in English translation. I hope that this reworked version allows ready
access to some of the nuances of this sophisticated
example of oral literature without altering the integrity of the original narrative. This version of "The Couple Befriended by the Moon" served as the basis for
the transcription of the narrative that appears, under
the same title, in the main body of this text.

Following the formatting style utilized in the transcription of the other narratives in *Stories That Make
the World, verses* are marked here by numbers and
designate specific morpheme clusters separated, usually, by a quotative suffix, *'tsəruk,* meaning "it is said"
or "he/she said." I have marked *scenes* with capital
letters. Each scene designates clusterings of verses—
usually three, four, or occasionally five in number—

linked to specific characters and their actions and qualities in a given locale. I have also identified recurring series of *pairings:* Pairings of scenes, verses, or actions are marked by a left brace ({); pairings of parallel and repetitive clusterings and of contrasting and antithetical clusterings are noted in brackets at the end of the pertinent verse or scene; and morphemes repeated within a given verse or scene are <u>underlined</u>.

Given the source text for "The Couple Befriended by the Moon," the storyteller's intonation and stress and the listeners' responses are not identified.

In my retranscription of Young Crane's story, I have made a number of modifications on the basis of linguistic and cultural considerations. For instance, I have added to the text the quotative suffixes that appear in Lowie's transcription of the Apsáalooke lined verses but not in his English translation. In conformity with the "future and nonfuture" verb tense characteristic of the Apsáalooke language, I have rendered the verb forms in present tense rather than the past tense used in Lowie's English translation. It seems to me to be a better rendering of the Apsáalooke language. In addition, I have, in a few instances, selected an alternative English translation for specific Apsáalooke words— for example, *acú·o,* "their lodge" as opposed to "their tent." And finally, I have recorded in italics the translations of the actual Apsáalooke words that appeared in the original text and hence were presumably spoken by Young Crane. Words implied but not overtly stated appear in roman type.

We begin by looking at the first two scenes, printed here in parallel Apsáalooke and English translations and with the verses numbered. Then we'll look at the entire text of the story in English only, with verses, scenes, and pairings of various elements marked as indicated above.

THE COUPLE BEFRIENDED
BY THE MOON
(YOUNG CRANE AS TOLD TO ROBERT LOWIE)

1. *apsá·ruk*   *hirékyo·*   *dú·o·'tsəruk.*
   Crows   this way   were coming.

2. *ambúako·n*   *awaxá·wɛ*   *kuc*   *dí·ru'tsəruk.*
   From below   mountain   towards   they walked.

3. *acɛwatsá·tsi'tsəruk.*
   A big camp was there.

4. *batsé·rək*   *tɛ·xiərək*   *úəwicí'tsəruk.*
   A man   did not see well;   he had a wife.

5. *isá·cgyuo·*   *hawátka·tdək*   *acú·o·*   *iəká·cka·tdək*
   Horses   only one;   their tent   was small

   ictcitsu·ka·k   *ictúka·tua*   *ictsitsú'ka·k.*
   one side of their pack   their meat,   they packed on one side.

6. *bí·əc*   *icbatsípbicdək*   *ba·parawi·'tsəruk.*
   The woman   had a digger   she was digging from time to time.

7. *dú·sa'pe·tarà·riek·*   *akbatsé·re*
   They went on one side of the camp   When someone hunted,

   ba·ce²   *batsá·tsit*   *duadiək*
   dead game   there was plenty;   they came.

   annútsisùa   *dútsikya·tseru'tsəruk.*
   to where it was killed.   they took some of it.

8. *karacé·c*   *icí·urək*   *dú·ra*   *dá·ckyɛn*
   The camp   had camped.   they came;   on the outside

   icí·o'tsəruk.
   they camped.

9. *batsé·sua*   *icé·rək*   *karakurá'ts'əxit*
   They were poor   very;   when all had left,

itcanná·ute   *dé·ru'tsəruk.*
where tracks went   they went,

10.   *tsiré*   *isá·cgyε*   *dú·xaci'kya·k*   *ba·pí'tsəruk.*
     Husband   her horse   she let hold,   she dug roots.

THE COUPLE BEFRIENDED
BY THE MOON

YOUNG CRANE, CROW (TRANSCRIBED FROM
LOWIE'S 1918 RENDERING)

A   1   *Crows off there* are *coming,*
              it is said.

    2   *From below towards the mountains* they are *walking,*
              it is said.

    3   *A big camp* is *there,*
              it is said.

{
B   4   *A man* who *does not see* very *well has a wife,*
              it is said.

    5   They have *only one horse;*
              their lodge is very small,
        {   they *pack on* only <u>*one side;*</u>
              their meat,
                  they *pack on* only <u>*one side.*</u>
        [lodge, packed on one side { meat, packed on one side]

    6   *The woman* with *a root digger* gathers *plants,* (roots)
              it is said.[3]

    {
    7   *They* are *on one side* of the camp;
              a hunter killed plenty of game;
        {   *they come to where* it is killed,
                 they *take some of it,*
                       it is said.[4]
        [plenty { some]
   [6: roots { 7: meat]
[A: Crows, big camp, well provided { B: poor couple, on the side of the camp,
blind, one horse, small lodge, little meat, roots]
C   8   *The people come* they *camp;*

{   *on the outside they* (husband and wife) *camp,*
        it is said.
[camp of people { camp of couple on the outside]

9   *They are very poor;*
        when all have left they go where tracks go,
        it is said.

10   *The woman lets her husband hold her horse,* (he can't hunt)
        she digs roots,
            it is said. (reiterates poverty, and shows her alone-
            ness, her separation from husband and camp; is she
            on a quest?)

{
D   11   *Then that Moon from where she comes <u>do not know</u>,* (introduces mystery)
        this woman (Moon) *comes,*
        it is said.

{
12   *Makes friend* of wife, (adopts as guardian spirit)
        it is said.
[11: Moon { 12: wife]

13   *This Moon is a woman,*
        her *dress is decorated with elk teeth,*
        it is said.

{
14   *How she* (Moon) *comes <u>do not know</u>;*
        way over there she takes a big blue-handled knife,
        it is said.
[13: elk-tooth dress { 14: big blue-handled knife]

15   *This from that one it <u>ought to know</u>,* (should know what has
occurred)
    {   but *this woman <u>does not know</u>,*
        it is said.
[ought to know { does not know]
[C: poor couple without kinsmen { D: moon with elk-tooth dress and big
blue-handled knife adopts wife]

E   16   *Then this woman* (wife) *comes there,*
        it is said.

{
17   *On one side of the road she* (Moon) *comes, arrives,*

it is said.

[16: wife { 17: moon]

18   *"Partner, look for someone* to work for you.
         {   *Your husband is nearly blind,"*
              she says.

[healthy someone { nearly blind husband]

{

F   19   *When the camp* (the people) *had camped,*
         {   *they* (husband and wife) *come, camp,*
             it is said.

[camp of people { camp of couple]

20   *Plenty of meat;*
         they (the people) *do not break camp.*

{

21   *She tells her husband,*
        "We are poor,
          I have been told to look for someone; (to work for
          you)
            over there Musselshell Forks (river) *there are*
            horses for you,"
              she says.

[20: plenty { 21: poor]

22   *"A roan* is *your mount;*
         also there a big-bellied mare."

[19 and 20: camp of people with plenty of meat { 21 and 22: poor
couple must look outside camp for plenty, Musselshell Forks]

[E: wife receives vision/medicine from Moon { F: wife conveys vision/medicine
to husband]

{

G   23   *Hidatsa there* are *camped.*[5]

24   *Then those that have no guns, powder, tobacco, horses with*
        them, *they take many,* (trading)
        it is said.

25   *Then they face uphill that is it,*
        it is said.

[F: Crows and poor couple look outside camp { Hidatsa and those without
look inside camp]

{

H   26   *This woman has some powdered <u>turnips</u>,*
        it is said.

{
27   *"Do it, make pudding from <u>turnips</u>,"*
          he says.

[26: has some powdered turnips { 27: makes pudding from turnips]

28   *This man:*
          "<u>Four</u> very brave young men, call them,"
          he says.

{
29   *Then this woman calls <u>four</u> of them,*
          they come,
               it is said.

[28: husband, call four brave men { 29: wife, calls in four brave men]

30   *Pudding she passes to them,*
          they eat,
               it is said.

[G: Hidatsa exchange, trading { H: couple exchange, pudding]

{
I   31   *This man* (husband),
          it is he.

32   *"Have your moccasins made,"* (to prepare for a journey)
          he says.

33   *"Musselshell Forks my horses are there,*
          let us go,"
          he says.

34   *This woman* (wife) *is smoking with them.* (acknowledges wife's role)

[H: couple invite four young men { I: husband tells of vision, journey, and horses]

J   35   *Then they <u>go out</u>,*
          they go,
               it is said.

36   *"When you have <u>gone out</u>, have moccasins made,"*
          they say. (husband/wife)

37   *These four young men <u>go out</u>,*
          there they meet,
               they speak,
                    it is said.

{
K   38   *<u>Two</u> of them are friends;*
     {   *the other <u>two</u> are the same,*

it is said.

[two are friends { two are same]

39   *"Come, what are you going to do about it?"*
        he says.

40   *These two:*
        "If he really has good medicine he would not be that sort
        of person."

{

41   *Then these other two:*
        "We with him will go,"
        they say.

[40: young men doubt man { 41: young men trust man]

42   *"They are poor,*
        it may be true;
    their faces they don't hide,
        it may be true."

43   *They go home,*
        have moccasins made,
            these young men,
                it is said.

[J: one group of four young men gather { K: divided into two pairs of young men]

L   44   *This woman (wife) cuts up the lodge cover,*
        she makes moccasins,
            it is said.

{

45   *"When you come your moccasins are ready,*
    we'll go that night,"
        she says to this man (husband).

[44: moccasins made { 45: moccasins given]

46   *The woman (wife) makes a padded saddle for her husband,*
        it is said.

{

47   *"When you bring horses, ride on this,"* (padded saddle)
        she says.

[46: saddle made { 47: saddle given]

48   *Then this woman, the Moon, gives her (wife) an hourglass-shaped bag,*
        it is said.

{

49   *They tie* it *there to the other side of the screen,*
             it is said. (the tipi liner within the lodge)

[48: bag received { 49: bag given]

{

M   50   *These young men when it gets dark,*
          "<u>We have come</u>,"
             they say.

     {

    51   *Those two* <u>went</u> *away that had said if he were good medicine*
he would not be *such a person,*
          these two (young men who came) *they tell them,*
          (husband/wife)
             it is said.

[50: two men who trust couple { 51: two men who do not trust couple]

52   "<u>We have come</u>,"
             they say.

()   *"There outside wait for me,*
          I am getting things ready,"
             he says. (husband)

{

53   *This man* <u>comes</u> *out,*
             it is said.

[52: young men { and 53: husband]

[L: wife prepares and gives gifts (moccasins, saddle, bag) { M: two young men and husband gather (and receive the gifts from the woman); the "medicine-consequence scenario"]

N   54   *Then this woman takes the bag,*
      {   *she goes out with her husband,*
           it is said.

     [woman { husband]

    55   *Her husband's saddle she has made;*
          she made him pack;
      {   *he packs,*
       he stands ready,
           it is said.

     [she { he]

    56   *"They come,"*
          she says;

()   *go farther with these* things,
          it is said.

57   This woman sings a glad <u>song</u>,
      it is said.

{

58   *A fine scout <u>song</u> also she sings,*
      it is said.

[57: glad song { 58: scout song]

59   *"That way go,*
    Musselshell Fork there this roan is coming,"
      she says.

{
O   60   *When it gets dark,*
    then they go,
      it is said.

61   <u>*Three*</u> *of them on the Yellowstone River kill,*
    eat of a very fat buffalo,
      it is said.

62   *"We <u>three</u> cannot keep, cook, eat up the meat,"*
    they say.

63   *All <u>three</u> have packs,*
    it is said.

64   *After they have cooked,*
    they do not build a fire,
      they will eat what remains,
        it is said.

[N: wife gives gifts (bag, saddle, songs, directions) for journey { O: three men receive gifts and with them, go on journey; repeat of "medicine-consequence scenario"]

{
P   65   *"Here is the Fork,"*
    they say.

66   *"Well, go.*
    I will stay here,
      <u>*bring horses,*</u>*"*
    he says.

67   *In a mountain valley there is a herd of horses close to this side;*
    <u>*bring*</u> *them,*
      it is said.

[O: journey to horses { P: arrive at horses]

{
Q   68   *"Look for the roan,"*

he says.

69 *When they look for it,*
    it is among them;
    they take,
        they lead it,
           it is said.

70 *They drive,*
    they bring it.

71 *This poor man they take it to,*
    it is said.

{
R   72 *"Here is the roan,*
    take it,"
        they say,
  ( )   *they give it to him,*
    it is said.

73 *The saddle he fixes,*
    on it he rides,
        it is said.

[Q: search for and bring back roan { give roan to husband]

{
S   74 *"Look for a big-bellied mare,"*
    he says.

75 *When they look,*
    it is among them,
        it is said.

76 *"Here it is,"*
    they say.
  ( )   *"Take it,*
    bring it,"
        he says.

77 *When they have brought it,*
    he fixes a rope,
    he leads it,
        it is said.

[Q and R: roan and saddle fixed to it { S: big-bellied mare and rope fixed to it; S combines Q search for horse with R giving horse to husband]

[P: husband with medicine gives directions to young men { Q, R and S: young men receive directions and bring the horses back to husband; repeat of "medicine-consequences scenario"]

T 78 *"Let them come,"*
     he says.
 ( ) *He goes;*
     they drive the horses behind him,
      it is said.
 79 *They come to Bull Hill,*
     below the mouth of Pryor Creek,
      they swim with their horses.[6]

[O: journey to horses { T: return with horses]

U 80 *Then:*
     "Those who are partners,
      I first with it (medicine) *find something,*
       you shall last do it,"
        they say. (the young men will now go separately with the aid of the man's medicine)

{
V 81 *Horses* there are *eighty.*
     These partners each have ten,
 { *this man sixty they give,*
     it is said.
  [partners { man]
 82 *These* people *some time:*
     "They have come with horses,"
     they say.
 83 *"That man is* really *it,"*
     they say. (the husband really has medicine)
 84 *All three have geldings.* (indicating three types of horses)

{
W 85 *When they get to the edge of camp,*
     this man cuts out his sixty he <u>*brought*</u>,
     it is said.
 86 *When this poor woman's husband comes with horses,*
     they buy a very large lodge,
      furnishings for it with the horses <u>*brought*</u>;
     they have something then,
      it is said.

[V: horses gained via medicine { W: large lodges and furnishings via horses and medicine]

[U: medicine acknowledged { V and W: benefits and consequences of medicine (horses, large lodge, furnishings); repeat of "medicine-consequences scenario"]

{

X   87   *In the meantime, <u>their lodge</u> is very large;*
          {   *these young men come inside, sing praise songs,*
                  they had it for <u>their lodge</u>,
                        it is said.
          [couple's lodge { young men's lodge]

      88   *This one young man:*
             "*With this Medicine I first shall go somewhere,*
                <u>four times</u> with it I <u>find something</u>." (the young men will go separately with the aid of the man's medicine)

      {
      89   *This other* young man *also <u>four times</u>, <u>finds something</u>,*
             it is said.[7]
      [88: one young man's medicine { 89: other young man's medicine]

{

Y   90   "*Look for someone* to work for you,"
             she says. (wife) (reiterate vision-medicine from Moon)
      91   *These also took pity on us,*
             they did it," (they really have medicine)
                she says. (wife) (the Moon had said this to the wife)

      {
      92   "*Two young men insulted us,*
             they don't do it," (they don't have medicine)
                she says. (wife)
      [91: young men who took pity on couple { 92: young men who insulted couple]
      93   "*When you go on a horse raid,*
             <u>*send*</u> *away from among you the two young men who did not go for us,*
                <u>*send*</u> *them home,*"
                      she says.

{

Z   94   *Young men go on a horse raid,*
             they bring horses,
                kill enemy,

they are very good,
it is said.

{
95   *They* (a group of young men) *go on the warpath;*
when they (the other two young men) *go,*
they are be sent away by themselves,
now they cry,
it is said.

[94: young men who bring in horses { 95: young men sent away and cry, horse not brought in]

96 *That is the end.*

[Y: two pairs of young men { Z: young men who insulted]

[X: medicine acknowledged { Y and Z: consequences of having and not having medicine; repeat of "medicine-consequences scenario"]

We can easily identify the "orphan quest" literary motif within this narrative. The man and the woman have no family; he is partially blind; they have only one horse, a small lodge, and "meat on one side"; and they "go on one side of camp." They are like orphans. While alone and away from camp (as if on a quest), the wife receives a vision and is adopted by a spirit guardian, the Moon. It is the wife who sacrifices her only lodge cover to make moccasins for the journey to find the horses. The two pairs of young men are themselves tested to see who has "sincerity" and who has doubt. The two who respect their elders regardless of appearances have their sincerity rewarded. The other two, the doubters, also receive their just rewards.

Note the interesting structural repetition of the "medicine-consequences scenario": medicine is acknowledged and given, and as a result of that medicine, benefits are gained. This motif is repeated in scenes: L { M; N { O; P { Q, R, S; U { V, W; and X { Y, Z.

It is intriguing, too, to note that the Moon, a spiritual guardian, adopts the couple. Yet she, the Moon, speaks only to the woman, who shares the message with her husband, who then leads the quest for the horses. It is the husband who is acknowledged as owner of medicine. Yet, why did the woman, and not the man, receive the vision? And why did the wife "smoke" with the men, a practice generally separated by gender? Is it an acknowledgment of the special relationship between the wife and the Moon, who is, after all, identified as a woman?

I

Appendix 2

Lesson Plan

*T*he following materials are provided to assist the teacher in presenting oral literature texts in a classroom setting. The lesson plan is generalized, and the teacher is encouraged to modify this plan to fit his or her particular classroom needs. The suggestions are adaptable for instruction in grades K–12 as well as on the college level.

Subject
Storytelling and Oral Literature: A Language Arts and/ or Social Studies Lesson Plan. This lesson plan is appropriate not only for presenting American Indian oral literature but also for presenting the oral literature of local homesteaders, miners, loggers, farmers, and/or members of Euro-American or any other ethnic family groups.

Appropriate grades
K–12 and beyond, with particular modifications for each grade level.

Objectives
The student will be made aware of
  1. The cultural world view, the historical events and personalities, and the literary values and creativity conveyed in the oral literature of the Inland Northwest region—that is, cultural themes, literary motifs, and purposes of a people's oral literature

2. The dynamics of traditional techniques of story-telling—that is, the art of storytelling, which should enhance the student's appreciation of oral literature
3. His or her own abilities as a storyteller, thus enhancing his or her abilities to communicate creatively with others and to use his or her imagination

Activity
The techniques of storytelling, the cultural and historical value of oral literature, and applications of storytelling will be explored through guest presentations by storytellers, teacher presentations, and class projects. Anticipate a minimum of four 90-minute in-class sessions comprising (1) a review of oral literature and storytelling functions and techniques, (2) presentation by a storyteller, (3) in-class analysis of the story's text and the storyteller's techniques, and (4) student storytelling of regional oral literature. In addition, students will conduct out-of-class oral literature research.

Procedure
First session: Review with the class the various types and functions of oral literature (as distinguished from oral history) as well as the techniques of storytelling. The review will introduce the subject and enable the students to better appreciate guest storytellers.

Second session: Invite a guest storyteller to class. Prepare an informal setting that is conducive to storytelling—for example, arrange desks or chairs in a semicircle or remove them entirely and have students sit on the floor. Avoid a "stage" situation—no podiums or microphones. Introduce the storyteller to students, offering biographical information and information about oral literature in general. As the stories are being shared, have the students pay attention to (1) the themes, characters, motifs, and humor conveyed in the stories and (2) the particular techniques used in the telling, for example, hand gestures, voice intonations, and sentence repetition. Encourage students not to interrupt unless the storyteller encourages some form of audience interaction. Thank your guest and have students send personal thank-you notes.

Third session: Review with the students the performance of the storyteller, discussing the characters, cultural themes, literary motifs, humor, and adventure found in the narrative and the special techniques used to present it. What new insights were gained into the history, personalities, and world view of your local area?

Now prepare the students for their own storytelling presentations. Review the general techniques of storytelling and those used by the guest storyteller. But emphasize that everyone has his or her own unique style, that there is no proper or improper style. Source material for the stories can be acquired in one of two ways. The teacher can collect stories (representing American Indian, pioneer, mining, or steamboat eras, for example) and hand out the examples to students.[1] Or preferably, students can research the oral literature for themselves. They can interview elders, family members, neighbors, and friends for examples of oral literature. Be sure *that proper permissions are obtained prior to the retelling,* and *that students exhibit a polite and courteous demeanor in their interviews.* Keep in mind the diversity of oral literature types. Students may elect to collect examples from a certain genre, for example, riddles or proverbs. Once each student has a story or a collection of materials, it should be reviewed by the teacher for appropriateness. Have the students practice telling their stories to family or friends, using the particular techniques of storytelling they have found most comfortable.

Fourth session: Have students present their stories in class. As with the guest storyteller, establish an informal atmosphere. After each presentation, review the story's content for historical and cultural significance. To avoid a competitive situation among students, you may not want to discuss aloud the student's storytelling techniques.

Follow-Up
Have students describe what they have learned about local history and personalities, about researching a story, about storytelling, and about their own involvement in the process. Did it spark their creative imaginations? Younger students can offer their comments verbally, recording them on paper or the blackboard. You can have students draw sketches of their own stories and stories of others, illustrating the characters and sequences of the stories. The sketches, along with the written stories, can be combined into a student book project. Older students can use the stories as example material for a creative writing exercise, combining the stories into a single narrative, or as an oral literature anthology project, collecting the individual stories so others can enjoy them.

Extensions
1. For older students, try videotaping the storytelling sessions in order to keep a record of both stories and storytelling techniques.
2. Start a storytelling group that will travel to other schools to share local oral literature.
3. Print a pamphlet of stories collected from your community. If you have enough good stories, have a book published.
4. Show students how stories from Europe, Africa, Asia, and Latin America have been incorporated into stories in the United States.
5. Have students share stories from their own cultural heritage as well as from other cultures. This might be done in the context of an ethnic meal in which students bring a food

from their own cultural heritage for a class
meal.

6. Link your class project with a drama class. The
stories your students have collected can be
recombined into a script for a theatrical production.

Storytelling Techniques: Some Additional Considerations

In addition to the techniques of storytelling suggested
by the Indian elders, let me offer the following general
considerations. They may be helpful in the presentation of your own as well as your students' stories in a
classroom situation:[2]

1. It is critical that you like the story you tell. It
must spark your interest and enthusiasm if it is
to do the same for your audience. Be familiar
with the story. Read and/or hear several versions if you can find them and choose the one
you like best.

2. Think of your audience when choosing a story.
Simple plots with lots of repetition are best for
younger audiences; more complicated twists
are appreciated by older children or adults.
Children may lose interest if words are too
difficult, but they love new words (especially
nonsense) and will often grasp the meaning
of unfamiliar words from the context of the
story.

3. Above all, practice! Some people like to do so
in front of a mirror or by taping the story and
playing it back. Others find it easier to practice while doing housework, riding in a car, or
exercising. I go over a story in my mind as I
take my morning run. Friends and family members can usually be persuaded to listen to a
story, although they can be more intimidating
sometimes than an audience of strangers. It is
much better to practice in front of others, al-

lowing the story to come to life through the participation of the listeners. As you learn the story, become cognizant of its overall structure and plot, the particular actions of its characters, and any specific verses that may be repeated throughout. However, do *not* try to memorize the narrative.

4. The most common mistake in telling a story is to go too fast. It is better to be too slow than incomprehensibly fast. If you make a mistake, correct it without apology or fuss—just as you would in ordinary speech. Remember, no one knows how the story is to be told except you. If you leave out a sentence or use it in a different place, proceed as if that is the way it should be. *You,* after all, are the storyteller. No *uh's*—there is nothing so deadening to a story. Pause if you must remember something, but don't say "uh." Try to be aware of any personal nervous habits or mannerisms that might be distracting to an audience.

5. Make eye contact with as many members of the audience as possible without shifting your gaze all over the place. The eyes of the listeners can be a window to their involvement with a story. Be aware of your listeners. If children are restless, shorten the story; speed up the pace; be more dramatic, emphasizing a word or a gesture; look the restless individuals right in the eye. Also be aware of where your audience is coming from. That is, what activity have they just been engaged in? Are they required to be at the storytelling session or did they elect to be there? Are they somewhat familiar with the content of the story itself or is this new territory for them? The very same story, told with the same enthusiasm, can be received in entirely different ways by different groups. The active participation of your audi-

ence will make or break the success of your storytelling. The listeners need to paddle the canoe.

6. Interruptions are inevitable. Inviting latecomers to be seated seems to work fine. If you have a deliberate troublemaker, try going up to the recalcitrant, even as you continue telling the story, and stare him or her in the eye. The message is usually effectively delivered this way. Try not to let little interruptions interfere with the flow. Just continue with your story, if possible.

7. Always consider your physical environment. Try to make it as informal as possible. Have students sit on the floor along with you perhaps, rather than at their desks. A formal setting can inhibit the participation of the listeners.

8. Give a little background for your story. Generally, the greater the story's cultural distance from the listeners, the greater the need for background. Attempt to anchor the story, which will allow quicker access to its interior.

a. Before beginning the story, ask what stories are used for, what their functions are (the context). Who were the teachers (the elders) and what were the textbooks (the stories) in traditional Indian societies of a hundred years ago? Discuss the importance of stories.

b. Before beginning the story, discuss some of its key literary motifs and themes (the text). What parallel motifs can be found in our own society? The orphan quest motif can be seen in the story of Cinderella, for instance. Try to link the listeners' own stories with one you are about to present.

c. Discuss how you first became acquainted with the story and/or why this particular story has meaning for you. Personalize the story.

d. Mention whether the story is still told

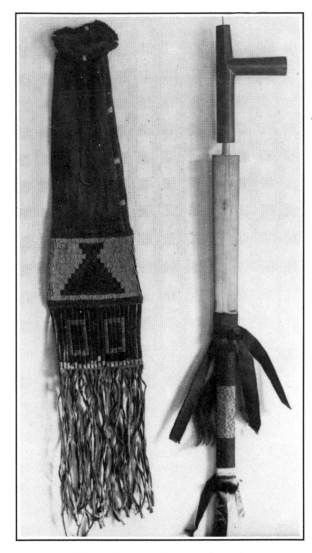

Nez Perce pipe and bag, ca. 1890. (Courtesy of the Idaho State Historical Society)

today—where, when, under what circumstances, and, most importantly, by whom. Whose story is it?

9. One strategy to involve the listeners in the story is to ask their assistance: "I need your help if this story is going to work. What are

the techniques that you see me using and what are the themes and lessons of the story?" Discuss them after the story.

10. Remember, your goal is to bring your listeners into the story as participants. You don't want passive observers. Re-member the story!

I

Notes

Preface

1. See "Lodge Boy and Throw-Away" in Lowie 1918: 74–98.

Introduction

1. Dundes 1966.

2. *Crow* and *Coeur d'Alene* are terms originally used by early fur traders to refer to these peoples. "Crow" may have been a casual translation of Apsáalooke, though "large-beaked bird" probably refers to a raven rather than a crow. As effective traders, the Schee-chu-umsh "drove a hard bargain" with the French traders, hence the French term *coeur d'alene,* "sharp-pointed hearts!"

3. For an overview of the contemporary Crow people, see Frey 1987. For excellent introductions to the peoples of the Plateau, see Hunn 1990, and of Idaho, see *Idaho Indians* 1990.

4. Phinney 1934: ix.

5. It is for this reason that I have elected to limit the number of photographs included in this text of the animals and birds alluded to in the narratives. I do not want in any way to encourage an automatic and exclusive association of the myth people with their physical counterparts. As will be discussed in reference to the techniques of storytelling used by the raconteurs, in providing only terse characterization, the reader's imagination is thus allowed to contribute to the imagery of the myth people, and the reader participates more fully in the unfolding story.

6. The $\mathcal{L}$ phoneme is similar to a "chu" sound, voiced with the tongue placed at the roof of the mouth.

7. The story of Four Smokes was told in English by Lawrence Aripa in April of 1991 to a live, non-Indian audience. This account is a transcription of recording and my own hearing of the story. I have included some of Lawrence's introductory remarks to the story.

8. *Moos-sim-mot* translates from the Coeur d'Alene as Four Smokes.

9. For additional discussion of these issues, see Hymes 1981; Kroeber 1981; Sherzer and Woodbury 1987; Swann 1983, 1987, 1992; and Tedlock 1983.

10. This account of "The Couple Befriended by the Moon" is based upon a retranscription of Robert Lowie's (1960:78–82) translation of the story as told by Young Crane. See Appendix 1 for an analysis and retranscription of this story.

11. The transcribed stories shared by Mari Watters and Basil White were also based on recordings derived from this project, which was sponsored by the Idaho Humanities Council and Idaho Mythweaver, Inc., under the guidance of Jane Fritz, project director.

12. For an excellent account of Tom Yellowtail's life, see his autobiography (with Michael Fitzgerald 1990). Also see Medicine Crow 1992:50–57.

The Text

1. For a comprehensive review of the cultural themes as reflected in Coeur d'Alene myths, see Reichard 1947.

2. For additional discussion of this concept, see Frey 1987.

3. This account is based upon the story as told by Louis Simpson, a Wishram, which appears in Sapir 1909:1–7. A man "about seventy or seventy-five years of age" when he told this story in 1905, Louis Simpson "implicity believes in the truth of all the myths he narrated," and that they were "not invented by himself, but have been handed down from time immemorial" (1909:xi). I have substituted the generally used "Sisters" for "women," which is found in the Sapir text. (The women are sisters to each other.)

4. The Columbia River.

5. The location where Coyote released the fish is now called Celilo Falls, on the Columbia River. The story establishes that the first salmon in the spring are to be announced by the arrival of the swallows. The narrative of Coyote releasing the Salmon is shared throughtout the Plateau region by such peoples as the Coeur d'Alene (Reichard 1947:98–105 and Teit et al. 1917:121), Colville (John Grim, personal communication 1991), Nez Perce (Aoki and Walker 1989:11–43; Phinney 1934:380; and Allen Slickpoo, personal communication 1991), Kootenai (Boas 1918:173–75), Sahaptin (Teit et al. 1917:139–44), Sanpoil (Ray 1933:173 and Teit et al. 1917:67–71, 101–103), Thompson (Teit 1898:27 and 1917:67–71), and Wasco (Sapir 1909:266–67).

6. *Du' lululu* gives the sound of thunder rumbling far off.

7. This account is based upon Jacobs' (1929:196–200) Klikitat story as told by Joe Hunt, an elderly medicine man. Hunt was frequently called by the few remaining Klilitat families of the neighorhood to doctor their sick. He was also a "lover of the 'bone-gamble' game". Joe Hunt lived in Husum, Washington (1929:242).

8. Coyote's speech is spoken with comic dignity in a characteristic quavering monotone.

9. In the plateau region, "Coyote and Swallowing Monster" is the most widely shared account of the "coming of the people." The narrative is told by the Coeur d'Alene (Reichard 1947:68–71; Teit et al. 1917:122; and Lawrence Aripa, personal communication 1991), Sahaptin (Teit et al. 1917:148–51), Thompson (Teit 1912a:314), and Wishram (Sapir 1909:41–43), for example. Additional accounts of the Nez Perce story appear in Phinney 1934:18–28 and Aoki 1979:23. This particular account is based on a recording (collected by Jane Fritz as part of an Idaho Mythweaver project) and my own hearing of the story as told by Mari Watters in August of 1991. Mari was born in 1934, the daughter of Samuel Watters, a well-known Nez Perce storyteller. She passed on in May of 1992. Depending on who tells the Swallowing Monster story, the last and bravest people to be made from the Monster is the storyteller's own people.

10. Because this account is based on a recording, several qualities relating to the actual storytelling are presented here. You will notice that the morpheme clusters in this story are rather lengthy. This is a reflection of Mari's style of telling. I have indicated by Mari's use of the conjunction *and*, the verses that are generally separated within the scenes, but these verses may not be indicated by her pauses.

11. The next seven verses are generally part of the story but were not told at this particular session.

12. "Seal Boy" is based upon an account appearing in Sapir 1909:259–60. The text that appears in Sapir's collection may be a "free translation," thus lacking much of the phrase structures that would appear in the original Wasco telling of the story. As a consequence, the verse patterns I have identified may not replicate those of the original storyteller.

13. For a discussion of the literary motifs, characters, and plot found in Coeur d'Alene oral literature, see Reichard 1947.

14. For additional discussion of the complex and multifaceted character of Coyote, see Bright 1993, Radin 1956, Ramsey 1977, and Toelken and Scott 1981.

15. This story was told by Lawrence Aripa in April of 1991 to a non-Indian audience. Because this account is based on a transcription of a recording and my own hearing of the story, I have been able to convey many qualities of the storytelling art here. For instance, special vocal and gestural emphases and audience responses are noted in parentheses.

16. This account of "Coyote and the Dart" is based on Yellow-brow's account, originally titled "The Old Man Coyote and His Dart" and recorded in Lowie 1935:119–21. One of Lowie's "chief informants," Yellow-brow was born around 1868 and lived in Lodge Grass, Montana. I suspect parts of Lowie's account are "free translations" from his field notes. I have used Coyote's more commonly referred-to companion, Little Fox, instead of "little coyote," which appears in Lowie's version. In two other versions that Lowie recorded 1918:23–25, Little Fox is able to make off

with Coyote's "ill-gotten goods." As in Plenty Hawk's "Burnt Face" story, I have placed all the verb forms in the present tense, though Lowie recorded them in the past tense. In translating Apsáalooke (Crow) into English I have found the present tense more appropriate, given the "future and nonfuture" verb tense form of the language. I have also removed most of the conjunctive *and*s from Lowie's text, since they are rarely used in the telling of a story in Apsáalooke. Since personal pronouns (he, she, it) are not distinguished in Apsáalooke, I have added the appropriate gender references in our Crow texts to facilitate accessibility.

17. An exclamation of ridicule.

18. This comment alludes to Coyote's history of deception and to his self-confidence, believing himself to be above the advice of others.

19. Ancient Man is a term used by Coyote to address himself.

20. "Coyote and the White Man" was told by Lawrence Aripa in April of 1991 to a non-Indian audience. This account is based on a transcription of a recording and my own hearing of the story. This story tells of a time when Coyote's transformative power is waning, a time of the coming of white people to Indian country.

21. Upon reading the transcript for this story, Lawrence pointed out that he had left out "an important part" and asked that this scene about the ice cream be put into the text.

22. This text is a transcription of a recording of the story as shared by Tom Yellowtail in June of 1993. Having just told the Burnt Face story the evening before, Tom wished to share a "war story." Throughout his telling, there was a certain excitement in Tom's face, particularly when he told of the deception perpetrated by Wise Man on the enemy. The story of Wise Man nicely illustrates the trickster motif expressed in a tale and carried forth into human action.

23. This particular account of "Burnt Face" is based on the text appearing in Lowie 1918:152–56. I suspect that while the overall structure of the narrative reflects its indigenous form, specific word phrases may be "free translations" from the original Apsáalooke text.

24. For the Crow, physical perfection is among the traits (or achievements) that allow an individual to reach adulthood. Disfigurement can inhibit a person from reaching this status.

25. In the account told by Tom Yellowtail, while Burnt Face was on the mountains, he spent his time building what is now known as the Bighorn medicine wheel. See the next story.

26. I first heard "Burnt Face" from Tom some fifteen years ago. This particular transcription is based on a recording made at his cabin east of Wyola, Montana, in June of 1993. Only a few of Tom's many expressive hand gestures are noted here.

27. The Mountain Crows are one of two major tribal groups, the other being the River Crows. The River Crows moved about the Yellowstone and Bighorn River

areas, while the Mountain Crows traveled the mountain areas to the south of those rivers.

28. The medicine wheel is about 250 feet in diameter, with a hub and some 27 spokes, all made of stone. The Bighorn mountain range is in Wyoming, just to the south of the Crow Reservation.

29. For another story about the Little People "adopting" an "orphan," see "Dwarf's Ward" in Lowie 1918:165–71.

30. Tom wanted to include this story to provide additional understanding of the awakkulé, the Little People. Tom told this story immediately after he had told "Burnt Face," as if it were a natural continuation of that story. As with Tom's other stories, I have noted here only a few of his many expressive hand gestures.

31. A male member of one's own (mother's) clan.

32. As with the story of the Little People, Tom wanted to share this narrative to provide further understanding of the "Burnt Face" story. The story of Little Head was told, following breakfast, the day after "Burnt Face" was shared.

33. The two men are seeking to count coups on the enemy and thus receive honors and become a "chief."

The Texture

1. For additional discussion of orality and literacy, see Goody 1977, 1986, 1987; Ong 1982; and Thomas 1992.

2. I am not taking Marshall McLuhan's "the media is the message" position here nor suggesting that the theme of transformation is somehow reducible to the medium. I am only proposing that the medium has an inevitable influence on what is revealed within the phenomenal world and, in turn, on how that world is viewed.

3. For a discussion of several additional general considerations in the telling of stories, see Appendix 2.

4. The seasonal appropriateness for retelling stories should be emphasized. Following the Crow tradition, Old Man Coyote stories should be told only during the winter season, while among the Coeur d'Alenes, Coyote can be heard year-round. In your own retelling of the stories, respect the particular tradition from which the stories emanate.

5. Hymes 1981.

6. Jacobs 1959:73.

7. This account is taken from Ray 1933:132. Jim James was chief of the Sanpoil, "a dignified, proud full-blood about fifty years of age" when this story was recorded in 1930 (1933:130). I suspect the text is a free translation of the original narrative. Italics are used here to highlight those instances when phenomena are spoken into being.

8. This account appears in Boas and Chamberlain 1918:247–49. Barnaby, a storyteller of the Upper Kootenai, was "a man about sixty years of age" when this story was recorded (1918:v).

9. Lawrence Aripa told this story in April of 1991 to a non-Indian audience. This transcription is based on a recording of that session and my own hearing of the story.

The Context

1. In addition to the oral literature, the mythic world is also made accessible through the vision quests, the sacred Winter Dances, and the Sun Dances. In these instances, the individual enters the mythic world on a very personal basis, adopted by a guardian spirit. Here spiritual power is gained, transforming that individual, and applied, effecting a cure. In the Winter Dances, the individual "dances" his guardian spirit, he becoming that being.

2. Jacobs 1934:x.

3. Ray 1932: 71–75.

4. Boas and Chamberlain 1918:v.

5. Ramsey 1977:xxx.

6. Phinney 1934:ix.

7. Toelken and Scott 1981:92.

8. This story was told by Lawrence Aripa before a non-Indian audience in March of 1991. When he shared the tale with me, he stressed that it was a "true story."

9. This account appears in Sapir 1909:257–59. It is most likely a "free translation" of the original Wasco narrative. For an insightful discussion of the significance of this story, see Ramsey 1983.

10. Hood River, a southern tributary of the Columbia.

11. This story appears in Boas and Chamberlain 1918:244–46.

12. A place in Tobacco Plains, Northwest Montana.

13. This text is based upon materials appearing in Aoki 1979:17–19. Harry Wheeler was born in the 1890s in Pendleton, Oregon, but he considered the area along the Clearwater River near Orofino, Idaho his home. While attending Carlisle Indian School in Carlisle, Pennsylvania, he roomed with Jim Thorpe, the famous athlete. Wheeler died in 1963.

14. Lawrence told me this story at his home in September of 1993. He felt this particular narrative would be "a good one to finish off" all the stories he had shared. For similar accounts of this narrative, see Reichard 1947:104 (Coeur d'Alene) and Ray 1933:174 and Teit et al. 1917:71 (Sanpoil).

15. Basil White told this story before a non-Indian audience in April of 1991. Basil was born "during the coldest part of the year" on February 15, 1926, at a traditional Kootenai village site near Bonners Ferry, Idaho. He continues to reside close by, on

what has become the Kootenai Reservation. Most of the stories Basil now tells were told to him "over and over and over" by his grandmother, Mary Sam. This story closely parallels an account told by Mission Joe, an Upper Kootenai, to Franz Boas in the summer of 1914 (Boas and Chamberlain 1918:72–83). The story can also be found among the Klikitat (Jacobs 1929:223) and the Pend d'Oreille (Teit et al. 1917:115). The motifs of the "war with the Sky People" and the "arrow ladder" can be found in an Okanagan story (Teit et al. 1917:85), while the arrow ladder motif can be found in a Coeur d'Alene story (Teit et al. 1917:126). We also see in Basil's story the widely shared "creation of the various peoples from the parts of the slain monster" motif.

16. Nelson is a town in British Columbia.

17. Columbia is a lake at the headwaters of the Columbia River in British Columbia. Windemer, Cranbrook, and Grasmere are towns in British Columbia; Eureka and Libby are in Montana.

Appendix 1

1. My text sources are Lowie's *Myths and Traditions of the Crow Indians* 1918 (15):186–88, *Crow Word Lists* 1960b, and, with primary reference, *Crow Texts* 1960a:78–82.

2. Literally, something dead.

3. Note that the language overall is rather terse, with few function words, such as prepositions (about, for, of, with) and conjunctions (and, or, but), which are typically used to express grammatical connection and relationship.

4. Note that the left brace between scenes A and B indicates that those two scenes are paired, even if in an antithetical way: the Crows have a big camp; on the other hand, the couple has only one horse and belongings enough to pack on only one side of that horse. Note further that the brace within verse 5 marks another pairing, contrasting the couple's lodge and their meat, linked with a parallel pairing: both packed on one side only. (The repetitious phrases within the verse are highlighted by underlining.) The brackets at the end of verses 5 and 7 are then used to group the identified pairings, whether of similar or dissimilar elements, within those respective verses. Finally, the bracketed phrases at the end of scene B summarize the identified pairings found within the linked scenes, A and B. The rest of the narrative text is marked in this same way in order to draw your attention to the significant features of this narrative.

5. Hidatsa are a Plains Indian people of North Dakota.

6. The entire narrative is anchored in a specific landscape known to the Crow; note the constant use of *there* and of terms naming familiar objects: mountain, mountain valley, Musselshell River, Yellowstone River, Bull Hill, Pryor Creek.

7. Note the use of *four*: four young men are called in by the husband; four gifts

are given by the wife to her husband (moccasins, saddle, bag, songs); and four times the two young men who helped the couple will "find something."

Appendix 2

1. If you wish to focus on American Indian oral literature, see the bibliography for a listing of Inland Northwest Indian texts. Among the sources that provide authentic narrative texts, I would suggest you begin your search with Aoki 1979 (Nez Perce); Aoki and Walker 1989 (Nez Perce); Boas and Chamberlain 1918 (Kootenai); Jacobs 1929 (Klikitat) and 1934, 1937 (Klikitat and Cowlitz); Lowie 1960a (Crow); Phinney 1934 (Nez Perce); and Robinson 1989 and 1992 (Okanagan).

2. For additional discussion on storytelling, see Egan 1986, Maguire 1985, and Sawyer 1942.

I

Glossary

Anagogic: Intuitive and mystically based; often referring to spiritual meanings hidden from normal experience and expressed symbolically and figuratively; not dependent on empirical evidence.

Equality: A central cultural theme involving the notion that all phenomena—animal, plant, human, and spirit—are inherently equal, that no one phenomenon dominates another.

Giveaway: An exchange of gifts among kinspeople. Gifts can also be given to nonkin, to friends. The importance of the exchange is not in the receiving of a valuable material gift, but in the bonding of kinship. Giveaways often celebrate a rite of passage or an achievement of some distinction. The gifts may include blankets, foodstuffs, and money.

Heuristic: Interpretative in character, stimulating further inquiry into the subject in question; descriptive of an approach to learning and knowledge that may not be validated empirically.

Kinship: As used here, a pivotal cultural theme involving the understanding that all phenomena—animal, plant, human, and spirit—are intrinsically united.

Meaning: A dominant cultural theme involving the understanding that meanings and archetypes are found in a world portrayed in visions and dreams, through guardian spirits, by listening to the world—by being attentive.

Medicine: The sacred spiritual power expressed in Apsáalooke (Crow) as *baax-pée* and in Coeur d'Alene as *súumesh;* the life force that animates the world and is sought in vision quests. An individual's medicine is often associated with a guardian spirit such as Eagle, Buffalo, Elk, Wolf.

Medicine bundle: A collection of sacred objects representing a person's spiritual power; not the source of power, but that through which prayer and power flow. Opened during prayer, the bundle can contain such objects as sweet grass, eagle feathers, a small leather effigy of a spirit animal.

Metaphoric: Expressed in symbolic and figurative terms; not dependent upon empirical evidence.

Canada geese near
the Kootenai River,
northern Idaho.

Morpheme: The smallest meaningful unit of speech, for example, Coyote, story, Rock.

Myth: A story considered true and sacred that provides meaning and archetypes for living; spoken narrative about a thing or person—for example, Coyote—whose actions bring forth and transform the world prior to the "coming of human peoples."

Orality: The form of communication characterized by a reliance on speech patterns and exemplified by Indian storytellers; contrasts with literacy; has significant implication in reference to the nature of meaning and knowledge.

Orphan quest: A dominant literary motif involving an impoverished individual adopted by a spirit guardian and made whole again after being judged worthy.

Rite of passage: A ritual celebrating and publicly marking the transition of an individual from one social or spiritual status to another; often associated with life changes—for example, from puberty to adulthood—and with initiation—for example, becoming a shaman or healer.

Scene: A designated clustering of verses relating to a specific action or locale within a story plot.

Spiritual transcendence: A central cultural theme involving the acknowledgement of a spiritual reality beyond the overt material world; the source of medicine and visions.

Sun Dance: A Plains Indian—for example, Crow—tribal ceremony of prayer, healing, vision seeking, and renewal; held during the summer months, involving three to four days of fasting and dancing as forms of self-sacrifice.

Sweat bath: A widely practiced ritual of prayer and spiritual cleansing held in a small, domed lodge; heated rocks and water provide steam as the vehicle for the prayer and the cleansing.

Tale: A spoken narrative about the world after the "coming of human peoples"; like myth, considered true and sacred.

Trickster: A literary character often personified as Coyote; a deceptive, foolish, and self-serving person.

Verse: Lines within the text of a narrative designating a specific morpheme cluster; often separated by a quotative suffix.

Vision quest: A ritual of prayer and self-sacrifice; often initiated because of an illness or affliction in one's family or the need to seek guidance for oneself. The quester goes to a distant mountain and there fasts from food and water for a prescribed number of days, often two to four.

I

Bibliography

Aoki, Haruo. 1979. *Nez Perce texts*. Berkeley: University of California Publications in Linguistics 90.

————, and Deward Walker. 1989. *Nez Perce Oral Narratives*. Berkeley: University of California Publications in Linguistics 104.

Aripa, Lawrence, and Bingo SiJohn, comp. and ed. by Rodney Frey. 1993. *Me-y-mi-ym: Oral literature of the Coeur d'Alene Indian people* (written text and videotape). Plummer, Ida.: Coeur d'Alene Tribe Culture Committee.

Barker, M. R. 1963. *Klamath texts*. Berkeley: University of California Publications in Linguistics 30.

Benedict, Ruth. 1923. The concept of the guardian spirit in North America. Memoirs of the American Anthropological Association 29.

Blind Mose Chouteh. 1983. How the sweathouse came to be (mimeographed copy of an oral transcription held in the archives of the Flathead Culture Committee of the Confederated Salish and Kootenai Tribes, Pablo, Mt.). Also in *The last best place: A Montana anthology,* eds. William Kittredge and Annick Smith (1988), 87–91. Helena, Mt.: Montana Historical Society.

Boas, Franz and A. Chamberlain. 1918. Kutenai tales. Washington, D.C.: Bureau of American Ethnology, *Bulletin* 49:1–387.

Bright, William. 1993. *A Coyote reader.* Berkeley: University of California Press.

Brown, Joseph Epes. 1982. *The spiritual legacy of the American Indian.* New York: Crossroads.

Brown, Joseph Epes, ed. 1953. *The sacred pipe: Black Elk's account of the seven rites of the Oglala Sioux.* Norman: University of Oklahoma Press.

Bullchild, Percy. 1985. *The sun came down. New York: Harper and Row.*

Charlo, Vic, and Zan Agzigian. 1991. Trickster at Dirty Corner (play). Dixon, Mt.

Davis, Leslie. 1965. Remnant forms of folk narrative among the upper Pend d'Oreille Indians. *Anthropology and Sociology Paper 31.* Missoula: University of Montana. Also in *The last best place: A Montana anthology.* eds. William Kittredge and Annick Smith (1988), 119–26. Helena, Mt.: Montana Historical Society.

Doak, Ivy. 1991. Coeur d'Alene rhetorical structure. *Texas Linguistic Forum 32: Discourse*. University of Texas at Austin, Department of Linguistics and Center for Cognitive Science, 43–70.

Dundes, Alan. 1966. Texture, text and context. *Southern Folklore Quarterly* 28(4): 251–65.

Egan, Kieran. 1986. *Teaching as story telling: An alternative approach to teaching and curriculum in the elementary school*. Chicago: University of Chicago Press.

Frachtenberg, Leo J. 1910–1911. *Molale text notebooks* 1–8. Washington, D.C.: Smithsonian Institution Press. (A transcript is in the Melville Jacobs Collection of the Manuscripts and University Archives Division of the University of Washington Libraries, box 89, folders 6–13).

Frey, Rodney. 1983. Re-Telling one's own: Storytelling among the Apsáalooke (Crow Indians). *Plains Anthropologist* 28:129–35.

———. 1987. *The world of the Crow Indians: As driftwood lodges*. Norman: University of Oklahoma Press.

———, and Dell Hymes. In press. Mythology. *Smithsonian Handbook of North American Indians, Plateau* vol. 14. Washington, D.C.: Smithsonian Institution Press.

Furst, Peter, and Jill Furst. 1982. *North American Indian art*. New York: Rezzoli.

Gill, Sam. 1982. *Native American religions: An introduction*. Belmont, Calif.: Wadsworth.

———. 1983. *Native American traditions: Sources and interpretations*. Belmont, Calif.: Wadsworth.

———. and Irene Sullivan. 1992. *Dictionary of Native American mythology*. Santa Barbara, Calif.: ABC-CLIO.

Goody, Jack. 1977. *The domestication of the savage mind*. Cambridge, Eng.: Cambridge University Press.

———. 1986. *The logic of writing and the organization of society*. Cambridge, Eng.: Cambridge University Press.

———. 1987. *The interface between the written and the oral*. Cambridge, Eng.: Cambridge University Press.

Grim, John. In press. Cosmogony and the Winter Dance: Native American ethics in transition. *Journal of Religious Ethics*. University of Chicago.

Grinnell, George Bird. 1972. *Blackfoot lodge tales*. Williamstown, Mass.: Corner House.

Hines, Donald. 1984. *Tales of the Nez Perce*. Fairfield, Wash.: Ye Galleon Press.

Hultkrantz, Ake. 1953. *Conceptions of the soul among North American Indians: A study in religious ethnology*. Stockholm: Ethnographical Museum of Sweden.

———. 1973. *Prairie and Plains Indians*. Leiden, Neth.: E. J. Brill.

————. 1979. *The religions of the American Indians*. Berkeley: University of California Press.

————. 1987. *Native religions of North America: The Power of visions and fertility*. New York: Harper and Row.

Hunn, Eugene, with James Selam and family. 1990. *Nch'i-Wama "The Big River" mid-Columbia Indians and their land*. Seattle: University of Washington Press.

Hymes, Dell. 1953. Two Wasco motifs. *Journal of American Folklore* 66:69–70.

————. 1966. Two types of linguistic relativity: Some examples from Amerindian ethnography. In *Sociolinguistics*, ed. W. Bright, 114–58. The Hague: Mouton.

————. 1975. Breakthrough into performance. In *Folklore: Performance and communication*, eds. Dan Ben-Amos and K. S. Goldstein, 11–74. The Hague: Mouton.

————. 1976. Louis Simpson's The desert boy. *Poetics* 5(2):119–55.

————. 1980. Verse analysis of a Wasco text: Hiram Smith's Atunaqa. *International Journal of American Linguistics* 46:65–77.

————. 1981. *"In vain I tried to tell you": Essays in Native American ethnopoetics*. Philadelphia: University of Pennsylvania Press.

————. 1984. Bungling host, benevolent host: Louis Simpson's Deer and Coyote. *American Indian Quarterly* 8:171–98.

————. 1990. The discourse patterning of a Wishram text, Coyote frees the fish. In *Collected works of Edward Sapir, vol. VII, Wishram texts and ethnography*. Berlin: Mouton de Gruyter.

Hymes, Virginia. 1956–present. Field work with speakers of Warm Springs Sahaptin, especially Verbena Green, Susan Moses, Ellen Squiemphen, Hazel Suppah, Linton Winishut.

————. 1987. Warm Springs Sahaptin narrative analysis. In *Native American discourse: Poetics and rhetoric*. eds. Joel Sherzer and Antony C. Woodbury, 62–102. Cambridge, Eng.: Cambridge University Press.

Idaho Centennial Commission. 1990. *Idaho Indians: Tribal histories*. Boise: Idaho Centennial Commission.

Jacobs, Elizabeth, told by Clara Pearson, ed. Melville Jacobs. 1990. *Nehalem Tillamook tales*. Corvallis, Ore.: Oregon State University Press.

Jacobs, Melville. 1929. *Northwest Sahaptin texts*. Seattle: University of Washington Publications in Anthropology 2.

————. 1934, 1937. *Northwest Sahaptin texts*. New York: Columbia University Contributions to Anthropology 19(1 and 2).

————. 1958. *The content and style of an oral literature: Clackamas Chinook myths and tales*. Chicago: University of Chicago Press.

————. 1958–59. *Clackamas Chinook texts, part 1 and 2*. Bloomington: Indiana University Press.

Kauffman, John, Jr. 1981. *According to Coyote.* (Play based upon Nez Perce and other Plateau myths and commissioned by the John F. Kennedy Center for the Performing Arts) Honolulu, Hawaii: Honolulu Theater for the Young.

Kroeber, Karl. 1992. *Retelling/rereading: The fate of storytelling in modern times.* New Brunswick, N.J.: Rutgers University Press.

Kroeber, Karl, ed. 1981. *Traditional literature of the American Indian.* Lincoln: University of Nebraska Press.

Kroeber, Paul. 1988. Rhetorical structure of a Kalispel narrative. Paper presented at American Anthropological Association Meeting.

Linderman, Frank. 1930. *Plenty Coups: Chief of the Crows.* Lincoln: University of Nebraska Press.

Lowie, Robert. 1918. *Myths and traditions of the Crow Indians.* Anthropological Papers of the American Museum of Natural History vol. 23. (Reprint with introduction by Peter Nabokov, Lincoln: University of Nebraska Press, 1993.)

———. 1922. *The religion of the Crow Indians.* Anthropological Papers of the American Museum of Natural History vol. 25.

———. 1935. *The Crow Indians.* New York: Holt, Rinehart and Winston.

———. 1960a. *Crow texts.* Berkeley: University of California Press.

———. 1960b. *Crow word lists: Crow-English and English-Crow vocabularies.* Berkeley: University of California Press.

McDermott, Louisa. 1901. Folk-lore of the Flathead Indians of Idaho: Adventures of Coyote. *Journal of American Folk-lore* 14:240–51. Also in *The last best place: A Montana anthology.* eds. William Kittredge and Annick Smith (1988), 83–86. Helena, Mt.: Montana Historical Society.

Maguire, Jack. 1985. *Creative storytelling: Choosing, inventing, and sharing tales for children.* New York: McGraw-Hill.

Marshall, Alan. 1985. "Prairie chickens dancing . . .": Ecology's myth. In *Idaho folklife: Housesteads to headstones,* ed. Louie B. Atteberg, 101–107. Salt Lake City: University of Utah Press.

Mattina, Anthony. 1985. *The golden woman. The Colville narrative of Peter J. Seymour.* Tucson: University of Arizona Press.

Medicine Crow, Joseph. 1992. *From the heart of the Crow country.* New York: Random House.

Miller, Harriet, and Elizabeth Harrison. 1974. *Coyote tales of the Montana Salish.* Rapid City, S.D.: U.S. Department of the Interior, Tipi Shop.

Mourning Dove, ed. by Heister Dean Guie. 1990. *Coyote stories.* With notes by L. V. McWhorter and introduction and notes by Jay Miller. Lincoln: University of Nebraska Press.

Nabokov, Peter. 1967. *Two Leggings: The making of a Crow warrior.* New York: Thomas Y. Crowell.

Nabokov, Peter, and Robert Easton. 1989. *Native American architecture*. New York: Oxford University Press.

Ong, Walter. 1982. *Orality and literacy: The technologizing of the word*. New York: Methuen.

Oswalt, Wendell. 1988. *This land was theirs: A study of North American Indians* (4th ed.). Mountain View, Calif.: Mayfield.

Palmer, Gary, Lawrence Nicodemus, and Lavinia Felsmen. 1987. *Khwi Khwe Hnlmik-hwlumkhw "This is my land."* Plummer, Ida.: Coeur d'Alene Tribe.

Phinney, Archie. 1934. *Nez Perce text*. New York: Columbia University Contributions to Anthropology 23.

Quintasket, Charles. 1990. Skunk. In Mourning Dove, *Coyote Stories,* ed. Heister Dean Guie with notes by L. V. McWhorter, introduction and notes by Jay Miller. Lincoln: University of Nebraska Press.

Radin, Paul. 1956. *The Trickster: A study in American Indian mythology*. New York: Crown.

Ramsey, Jarold. 1977. *Coyote was going there: Indian literature of the Oregon country*. Seattle: University of Washington Press.

———. 1983. "The hunter who had an elk for a guardian spirit" and the ecological imagination. In *Smoothing the ground: Essays on Native American oral literature,* ed. Brian Swann, 309–22. Berkeley: University of California Press.

Ray, Verne. 1932. *The Sanpoil and Nespelem: Salishan peoples of northwestern Washington*. Seattle: University of Washington Publications in Anthropology 5.

———. 1933. Sanpoil folk tales. *Journal of the American Folk-Lore Society* 46:129–87.

Reichard, Gladys. 1947. *An analysis of Coeur d'Alene Indian myths*. Philadelphia: Memoirs of the American Folklore Society 41.

Robinson, Harry, comp. and ed. by Wendy Wickwire. 1989. *Write it on your heart: The epic world of an Okanagan storyteller*. Vacouver: Talonbooks/ Theytus.

———. 1992. *Nature power: In the spirit of an Okanagan storyteller*. Seattle: University of Washington Press.

Sapir, Edward. 1909. *Wishram texts*. Leyden: Publications of the American Ethnological Society 2.

Sawyer, Ruth. 1942. *The way of the storyteller*. New York: Penguin Books.

Schaeffer, Claude. 1949. Wolf and Two-Pointed Buck: A Lower Kutenai tale of the supernatural period. *Primitive Man* 22:8–22. Also in *The last best place: A Montana anthology,* eds. William Kittredge and Annick Smith (1988), 8–22. Helena, Mt.: Montana Historical Society.

Sherzer, Joel and Anthony Woodbury, eds. 1987. *Native American discourse: Poetics and rhetoric*. New York: Cambridge University Press.

Slickpoo, Allen, Sr., Leroy Seth, and Deward Walker, Jr. 1972. *Nu mee poom tit wah tit (Nez Perce legends).* Lapwai, Ida.: Tribal Publications.

Spencer, Robert et al. 1977. *The Native Americans: Ethnology and background of the North American Indians.* New York: Harper and Row.

Spier, Leslie. 1930. *Klamath ethnography.* Berkeley: University of California Publications in American Archaeology and Ethnology 30.

Spier, Leslie, and Edward Sapir. 1930. *Wishram ethnography.* Seattle: University of Washington Publications in Anthropology 3.

Spinden, Herbert. 1908. *The Nez Perce Indians.* Memoirs of the American Anthropological Association 11(3). (Reprint: Millwood, N.Y.: Krause Reprint, 1974.)

Stern, T. 1953. The Trickster in Klamath mythology. *Western Folklore* 12 (3): 158–74.

———. 1956. Some sources of variability in Klamath mythology. *Journal of American Folklore* 69:1–9, 135–46, 377–86.

———. 1965. *The Klamath tribe.* American Ethnological Society Monograph 41. Seattle: University of Washington Press.

Sturtevant, William, ed. 1978–1986. *Handbook of North American Indians* vol. 5, Arctic; vol. 6, Subarctic; vol. 8, California; vol. 9, Southwest; vol. 10, Southwest; vol. 11, Great Basin; vol. 15, Northeast. Washington, D.C.: Smithsonian Institution Press.

Swann, Brian, ed. 1983. *Smoothing the ground: Essays on Native American oral literature.* Berkeley: University of California Press.

———. 1987. *Recovering the word: Essays on Native American literature.* Berkeley: University of California Press.

———. 1992. *On the translation of Native American literatures.* Washington, D.C.: Smithsonian Institution Press.

Tedlock, Dennis. 1972. *Finding the center: Narrative poetry of the Zuni Indians.* New York: Dial.

———. 1983. *The spoken word and the work of interpretation.* Philadelphia: University of Pennsylvania Press.

Tedlock, Dennis, and Barbara Tedlock, eds. 1975. *Teachings from the American earth: Indian religion and philosophy.* New York: Liverright.

Teit, James. 1898. *Traditions of the Thompson River Indians of British Columbia.* Memoirs of the American Folk-Lore Society 6.

———. 1900. *The Thompson Indians of British Columbia.* Memoirs of the American Museum of Natural History 11(4).

———. 1906. *The Lillooet Indians.* Memoirs of the American Museum of Natural History 9(5).

———. 1909. *The Shuswap.* Memoirs of the American Museum of Natural History 4(7).

———. 1912a. *Mythology of the Thompson Indians.* Jesup North Pacific Expedition Publication 8(2).

———. 1912b. Traditions of the Lillooet Indians of British Columbia. *Journal of American Folk-Lore Society* 25:287–371.

———. 1930. The Salishan tribes of the western plateau. *Annual Report of the Bureau of American Ethnology* 45:23–197, 295–396, 447–758.

Teit, James, Marian Gould, Livingston Farrand, and Herbert Spinden, ed. by Franz Boas. 1917. *Folk-tales of Salishan and Sahaptin tribes.* Memoirs of the American Folk-Lore Society 11.

Thomas, Rosalind. 1992. *Literacy and orality in ancient Greece.* Cambridge, Eng.: Cambridge University Press.

Thompson, Stith. 1929. *Tales of the North American Indians.* Bloomington: Indiana University Press.

Toelken, Barre. 1987. *The dynamics of folklore.* Boston: Houghton Mifflin.

Toelken, Barre, and Tacheeni Scott. 1981. Poetic retranslation and the "pretty languages" of Yellowman. In *Traditional literature of the American Indian,* ed. Karl Kroeber, 65–166. Lincoln: University of Nebraska Press.

Turner, Nancy, Randy Bouchard, and Dorothy Kennedy. 1980. *Ethnobotany of the Okanagon-Colville Indians of British Columbia and Washington.* Victoria: British Columbia Provincial Museum 21 (Occasional Paper Series).

Turney-High, Harry. 1937. *The Flathead Indians of Montana.* Memoirs of the American Anthropological Association 48.

———. 1941. *Ethnography of the Kootenai.* Memoirs of the American Anthropological Association 56. (Reprint: Millwood, N.Y.: Krause Reprint, 1974.)

Vogt, Hans. 1940. *Kalispel language.* Oslo: Det Norske Videnskaps Akademi.

Walker, Deward. 1970. *Systems of North American witchcraft and sorcery.* Moscow: University of Idaho.

Walker, Deward. 1980. *Myths of Idaho Indians.* Moscow, Ida.: University Press of Idaho.

Wildschut, William. 1975. *Crow Indian medicine bundles* (vol. 17). New York: Museum of the American Indian, Heye Foundation.

Wissler, Clark. 1912. *Ceremonial bundles of the Blackfoot Indians.* Anthropological Papers of the American Museum of Natural History 7.

Wissler, Clark, and D. C. Duvall. 1909. *Mythology of the Blackfoot Indians.* Anthropological Papers of the American Museum of Natural History 2.

Woodcock, Clarence, ed. 1979. *Stories from our elders.* Pablo, Mt.: Flathead Culture Committee, Confederated Salish and Kootenai Tribes.

Yellowtail, Thomas, as told to Michael Oren Fitzgerald. 1991. *Yellowtail: Crow medicine man and Sun Dance chief.* Norman: University of Oklahoma Press.

Kootenay Lake, British Columbia.

Zenk, Henry, with comments by Howard Berman. 1992. Battle of the mountains. (Manuscript) From Leo J. Frachtenberg, *Molale text notebooks* (notebook 4). Washington, D.C.: Smithsonian Institution Press.

I

Index

Verse, 21–22, 217, 251